THE *W*rite Approach

Techniques for Effective Business Writing

THE *Write* Approach
Techniques for Effective Business Writing

Olivia Stockard, Ph.D.
Stockard-Elmer & Company, Inc.
New York, New York

Academic Press

San Diego   London   Boston   New York   Sydney   Tokyo   Toronto

Academic Press
a division of Harcourt Brace & Company
525 B Street, Suite 1900, San Diego, California 92101-4495, USA
http://www.apnet.com

Academic Press
24-28 Oval Road, London NW1 7DX, UK
http://www.hbuk.co.uk/ap/

Library of Congress Catalog Card Number: 98-89315

International Standard Book Number: 0-12-671545-9

PRINTED IN THE UNITED STATES OF AMERICA
99 00 01 02 03 04 QW 9 8 7 6 5 4 3 2 1

CONTENTS

CHAPTER 3
Developing the Document's Structure

CHAPTER 4
Principles of Readability

CHAPTER 5
Clarifying Your Voice

CHAPTER 6
Purpose and Vocabulary

CHAPTER 7
Straight Talk

CHAPTER 8
Tone

CHAPTER 9
Using Formatting Techniques

CHAPTER 10
Using Graphics

Introduction

I have written this book for the person who has already acquired a sense of good writing and now needs to develop it for business writing.

You probably first became acquainted with good writing when you were in school. You have read a number of novels, essays, and, possibly, texts of a highly technical nature. You may enjoy reading poetry. Undoubtedly, you read newspapers and magazines frequently.

My point is, you read a lot. Therefore, you are likely to have gained a concept of good writing, whether you're especially conscious of it or not.

You also know how to write sentences and paragraphs. The terms used in grammatical analysis may elude you, but you know a sentence from a nonsentence and writing that makes sense as opposed to nonsense. You have also probably had to write your share of academic projects and perhaps even a thesis.

Why, then, do you need this book? You need this book because many business people forget to apply the same standards of writing they learned in school to the writing they do on the job. Why this happens is a mystery to me. After all, whether you're writing on paper or on a computer, whether you're writing an essay or a business proposal, you're still *writing*. One purpose of this book is to clarify some of the confusion I have encountered about what makes business writing effective and persuasive.

Unlike some books about business writing, this one will *not* tell you that you have to unlearn everything you learned in academic writing classes to be a good business writer. Those classes gave you the right foundation. If you were able to write literate essays and reports in school, you will be able to write any type of business report or correspondence required of you. This book will help you learn how to apply many of the principles and techniques you already know to business writing.

Unfortunately, your worst stylistic models are likely to be some of the routine reports and correspondence that cross your desk and computer screen every day. The same bad habits get passed down from generation to generation, especially in large corporations. You'll need to develop some standards of taste before you can decide what is worth imitating in your colleagues' writing and what isn't.

The examples presented in this book are primarily drawn from paper and electronic documents written in large corporations and small businesses. You will be given the opportunity to confront some of this actual business writing, to react to it, and to edit it. You will also produce some writing of your own. Using my discussions of other people's work, you will be asked to make judgments and set your own standards. This is ultimately what every writer must do for himself or herself.

I encourage you to use this book to form your own concept of style—one that makes sense to you, given your audience and the situations you'll be writing about.

CHAPTER 1

What Is "Effective" Business Writing?

The Purpose of Business Writing
What Is "Effective" Business Writing?
What Do Business Readers Like?

THE PURPOSE OF BUSINESS WRITING

Business people write for a definite, practical purpose. That purpose is often different from the purposes of other types of writers.

Fiction writers write to entertain us. When we write letters to friends, we sometimes express our ideas and feelings much more freely than we would in a letter or memo to a business associate. Diary writers write to express their most personal feelings. In most cases, they do not expect their writing to be read by others and therefore they can take liberties with organization, vocabulary, and even grammar.

The goal of most business letters, reports, and memos, however, is to communicate information clearly to someone who needs that information for the purpose of doing business. Most business documents also require some kind of response from the reader, for example, to call the writer to discuss something, to make a decision on something the writer has proposed, or to sign off on a recommendation.

Even if the document's only purpose is to report information to the reader or to record some kind of progress that has been made, the writer expects that the reader or readers will use the information the document presents to help them do their jobs or to carry out some aspect of the company's business.

In short, you want the business reader to know some vital information or to be able to do something when he or she has finished reading your document.

When you determine your purpose in a particular business writing situation you will grapple with three key issues:

1. What is my message?
2. To whom is my message directed?
3. How do I want to deliver my message to my intended audience?

The first question requires you to determine the content of what you want to say. Choosing the content involves deciding the priorities you should assign to your key points—that is, the order in which you will present your ideas. The logic of your presentation will ultimately be determined by identifying the intended readers or audience for that message—the answer to question two.

The third question requires you to decide how to say your message in a way that will resonate with your intended audience. Your written voice must also serve your purpose, whatever you determine it to be—persuading, informing, analyzing, recommending, discussing, and so on.

Determining the answers to these three questions requires *thinking,* which is where the process of writing begins. Although there are templates suggesting logical approaches available to you and types of questions you should answer to determine who your audience is and what they need or want to know, these aids are no substitute for your own brain.

You will now have the opportunity to read and react to three short memos, all about the same subject. At the end of this activity, you will begin making your own decisions about what makes business writing "work."

BUSINESS WRITING THAT WORKS

Read the following three short reports. Decide which of the three communicates its purpose most clearly to you if you were the intended reader. A worksheet is provided after the three examples on which you may jot down your decision and your reasons for it.

REPORT No. 1

March 5, 1998

TO: Angela Jamison

FROM: Claire Lewis

SUBJECT: <u>History Envelopes</u>

On February 2, 1998, you asked me to place an order for 5000 history envelopes with the Purchasing Department to be received by March 1, 1998. I submitted the order to Ruth Roman in Purchasing on February 4, 1998. On February 28, I called to confirm delivery of the envelopes. I was told that Ruth Roman was on vacation and no one else could help. After discovering the name of the supplier, the Eaton Company, I called them and found out that they did not have a record of the order. I assumed that the history envelopes would arrive on time. Therefore, I did not take any further action. Unfortunately, the envelopes did not arrive on the date you requested.

REPORT No. 2

March 5, 1998

TO: Angela Jamison

FROM: Susan Allen

SUBJECT: History Envelopes

On February 4, 1998, I sent a purchase requisition to Ruth Roman in Purchasing, ordering 5000 history envelopes. I made it clear on the order that I had to have these envelopes by March 1, 1998.

On February 28, 1998, I called Ruth Roman to confirm delivery of the 5000 history envelopes on March 1, 1998. I was then told that Ruth Roman was on vacation and no one else could help me.

Then I remembered we had an old box of envelopes. So I checked the outside of the box and found the vendor's name. I called them, explaining my situation, and they told me they had no record of my order.

So I have now called and written a memo to the Department Manager of the Purchasing Department wanting an explanation on the status of my order.

REPORT No. 3

March 5, 1998

TO: Angela Jamison

FROM: Betty Davis

SUBJECT: Update on History Envelopes

As of today's date, the 5000 history envelopes I ordered from the Purchasing Department on February 2 have not arrived. Here is the sequence of events of the order:

- I ordered the envelopes on 2/2/98 for delivery no later than 3/1/98.
- On 2/4/98, I submitted the required purchase order to Ruth Roman in Purchasing.
- To confirm the delivery, I called Ruth Roman on 2/28/98 and was informed that no one had a record of the order.
- I then proceeded to contact Eaton Company, the supplier. They also had no record of the order.

I have taken no further action on this order. Please let me know what my next step should be.

Worksheet: Business Writing That Works

In the space provided, write the number of the report you thought made its purpose the clearest.

[   ] Report number

Jot down two or three reasons for your decision.

1. _____

2. _____

3. _____

WHAT IS "EFFECTIVE" BUSINESS WRITING?

Thousands of people in my corporate business writing seminars have completed the preceding activity. I would like to share with you their responses.

The overwhelming majority of readers selected example three, for the following reasons:

- The title identified the document's purpose.
- The first paragraph stated the writer's key message.
- The prose style and format helped them read the document with ease.
- The closing told them how the writer wanted them to respond.

A small number of readers preferred number two. Their reasons were:

- The paragraphs were short and readable;
- The closing described an action plan the writer would use to get results.

The majority of readers who did *not* prefer report 2 noted:

- The main message was never stated clearly, but only implied (i.e., the ordered envelopes had not arrived).
- The writer included extraneous information that readers would not need or want to know—specifically, how the writer found the address of the company from which the envelopes were ordered.
- The writing style narrated rather than reported the information.

No one has ever preferred example one. Readers have disliked this report for the following reasons:

- The main message is not revealed until the last sentence.
- The writer narrates the events in a rambling, unfocused way.
- The sentences are long and lose the reader's interest.
- There is no formatting to help readers follow the report's narrative "by eye as well as by logic."

At this point in a seminar, I ask the class to reflect on the implications of their responses and to form some principles of effective business writing based on their responses. In other words, what do business readers like in written documents? How do they prefer that business documents be written?

You have probably already arrived at some answers to these questions based on your own analysis. But let me share how most of my students responded.

WHAT DO BUSINESS READERS LIKE?

Business readers like:

- To know why you are writing to them (i.e., your purpose)
- To grasp your message easily and, usually, immediately—that is, in the first paragraph(s) and, if possible, in the subject title
- To follow the logic you use to support your main points
- To read your prose style easily, without confusion or rereading
- To know what action you want them to take in response to your message

At the end of this activity, seminar participants realize that they already know what makes this kind of writing "work." At this point, they are about one hour into the class. Everything they will study in more depth has been uncovered.

Is the class now over? The participants, like you, have known all along what makes business writing work. Why? Because, like you, they read this kind of writing and do this kind of writing a lot. The standards to strive for are already "unconsciously" learned from their everyday experiences.

However, the examples that started the class, and which you have just read, typify many documents routinely produced in business. They were not selected for discussion because they are particularly good or bad. They were selected because they are characteristic of the way many people in business write.

Therefore, the puzzling question many people face is that even though they know what they ought to do to write effectively for business, they are not always doing it. What could produce this paradox?

The answer, I believe, comes down to two things: thinking and technique. Many people simply do not take the time to think through the answers to the key issues of writing that were stated earlier.

1. What is my message?
2. To whom is my message directed?
3. How do I want to deliver my message to my intended audience?

The opening chapters of this book explore how the writer's choice of an organizational structure for a document reflects the answers to these key questions. Becoming conscious of how you think versus how you *present* your thinking enables you to identify and deliver your message coherently and persuasively to your intended readers.

The final chapters of this book invite you to grapple with creating a lively written voice. Business writers must engage their readers. Although they may not engage the reader in exactly the same ways as creative writers, business writers must still reach out and capture the reader's attention. Doing this means consciously choosing and applying stylistic and formatting techniques. Again, this book will ask you to examine various techniques and decide for yourself if, when, and how to use them.

CHAPTER 2

Organizing Business Documents

Organizational Patterns
Opening Strategies: Leads and Hooks
Frontloading and Signing Off
A Word about E-Mail
Inductive versus Deductive Logic

ORGANIZATIONAL PATTERNS

In writing, the first tangible evidence of your thinking is the pattern of organization you choose to communicate your thinking. The pattern you choose will reflect your decisions about:

- Your purpose for writing.

  Have you told readers *why* you are writing to them?

- Your understanding of readers' needs and interests.

  Does the sequence of ideas and information in your organizational pattern match your readers' priorities?
  Have you told them what they want to know in the sequence that matches their priorities?

- Your key messages.

  Have you identified and articulated your most important ideas clearly?
  Will your reader agree that they are the most important ideas?

There are different ways to organize any document. The pattern you choose, however, should match your *readers'* needs. After all, your overriding purpose in business writing is *communication*. Communication only happens when the intended receiver of a message (the reader) successfully receives it.

The two most common patterns for organizing business documents are "most important to least important" order and "analytical" order. By understanding the advantages and disadvantages of each, you will be able to choose the one that will communicate your purpose and message best to your intended readers.

"Most Important to Least Important" Order

One pattern of organization business writers often use is "most important to least important" order. In this pattern, you open with your most important message and work down to less important supporting messages. You first state your main points and summarize the reasons that explain those points in an opening paragraph or paragraphs. The reasons are then reiterated and developed more fully in the body of the document.

Most business readers and writers prefer most important to least important order because it is easy to read. Busy readers may not choose to read the entire document, but this kind of organization ensures that they will be able to see your main points immediately.

This pattern may be diagrammed as a pyramid. At the summit stands the message you have determined to be crucial in serving your readers' needs and interests.

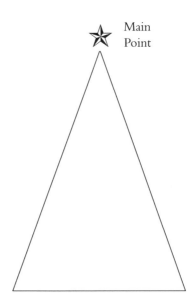

Main
Point

Advantages

Most important to least important organization is effective for

- Summaries
- Memoranda
- Formal reports
- Proposals
- Letters requesting information
- Letters replying to requests for information
- E-Mail

These forms of communication all have one thing in common: the writer must get to the point quickly and clearly.

Of the three reports you read in Chapter 1, only Report #3 used the pattern of most important to least important order. The writer stated the main message in the first sentence. Then she stated a chronology of events that explained the main message and used formatting to make the parts of the chronology stand out.

Disadvantages

If your goal is to communicate your ideas in writing clearly and efficiently, there are no disadvantages to most important to least important organization. Most of your business writing will likely use this pattern. Why? Business readers are generally impatient to get on with their work and like to know your most important messages right away. A frequent request of business people is, "Just give me the bottom line."

If, however, you are writing to readers who you know disagree with your message, your best strategy may be not to begin with it. If you do, readers may turn off or think they know your argument before they hear it. Similarly, if you want to convey bad news to your readers, this pattern of organization may be too hard-hitting. You may have to start with the reasons for the bad news and guide readers more slowly to your conclusions.

ANALYTICAL ORDER

Another pattern of organization commonly used derives from *inductive* logic: the process of reasoning from specific instances to general conclusions.

In this pattern, the writer requires the reader to follow a trail of logic and analysis, sometimes a chronology of events, before receiving the bottom-line message toward the end of the document. An introduction foreshadows the document's conclusion or gives the reader a structure for understanding how and why the document is organized as it is.

Main
Point

Because this pattern builds to its key message, it requires readers to follow the writer's trail of information and reasoning. The following diagram depicts the idea of this pattern as a trail.

When this pattern is used successfully readers are motivated to follow the path the writer determines. And the end of the trail is logical, even inevitable. Readers are not surprised when the key message reveals itself, for they have been led surely and persuasively to it.

Advantages

Analytical order is most appropriate for

- Research reports
- Letters or reports that contain a message the reader will perceive as provocative or sensitive
- Reports written to a hostile audience

In these situations, you must explain your reasoning process first to enable readers to understand the bottom-line message or accept an idea that they may not be sympathetic to.

You would generally choose analytical organization when you know you must work through your case slowly and in some detail to gain the reader's acceptance of your message.

Disadvantages

You'll often see business documents written in analytical order because writers have a tendency to write in the way they experience. Writers may organize the document in the way they thought through a problem or prolong presentation of the main points until all of the evidence is presented first. Sometimes they reproduce the order in which a series of events occurred (a *chronology*).

Readers, however, often find this kind of organization frustrating because they aren't sure of the document's direction. They may also have to plow through more detail than is necessary to understand the writer's message. For example:

> The overhead roll-up door at the South Loading Warehouse was 32 feet wide by 20 feet high, in three sections, with sliding vertical structural steel guides separating each of the sections. The center section was 14 feet wide and motor-operated. The side sections were chain-operated. Damage to the sliding vertical guides occurred when they were struck by vehicles using the center opening. This damage caused the side wind locks which run in the vertical guides to fall when buffeted by high winds. The center section along with the vertical guides was so badly damaged that the entire door was made inoperable. Therefore, it was removed by station forces and closed up with wood construction. There is a removable section in this wood closure to accommodate small vehicles. However, when there are large loads to be accommodated, the entire closure must be carefully removed and then re-installed, taking three hundred man hours to accomplish the work. In the interim while the closure is removed, the interior of the plant is exposed to the weather. The present wood closure which is combustible is subjected to steady deterioration, creating a safety hazard in high winds. Installation of a single heavy-duty, motor-operated roll-up door will allow entrance of large trucks without damage to the door. The door can be rapidly closed after trucks have entered, reducing the likelihood of freezing in cold weather.

Although the writer has a good recommendation to make, readers may not be motivated to stay with the report long enough to gain it. As so often happens, the writer prolonged presentation of the main point until the end. Additionally, the writer provides no way to help the reader assimilate the mass of detail presented at the beginning.

OPENING STRATEGIES: LEADS AND HOOKS

All writers must capture their readers' attention at the beginning of a document. Two methods of doing this are particularly useful for business writers. One method is writing an opening that *summarizes* the document's message. This kind of opening has long been practiced by newspaper writers and is called the *lead*. Another method is to *whet the readers' appetite* at the beginning so that they will want to read the entire report to glean the bottom-line message at the end. I call this kind of opening the *hook*.

SUMMARIZING THE STORY: THE LEAD

Journalists are always careful to summarize the most significant information *first* in a news story. To ensure a proper news summary, they are trained to answer the questions *who, what, when, where,* and *why* at the beginning. A common news lead might read:

> John K. Smitherson, Chairman of the Advanced Securities Trading Corporation, jumped off the roof of the Highland Motel in downtown Manhattan after his company lost five million dollars in today's stock market crash. He was dead on arrival at Bellevue Hospital.

If you want to find out, you must read the body of the story to learn the gory details.

The lead is an efficient way of helping the reader quickly grasp the central facts of a story. This method may also be used by report writers, although the content of the lead in business reports will not always be strictly factual. When the report writer summarizes his or her bottom-line message at the beginning, it can be a conclusion, a recommendation, a decision, or a judgment. The body of the report presents facts, evidence, and logical arguments in support of the main point or points. The report usually ends with the writer asking for a response or follow-up from the readers as a result of their having read the report.

The report on the roll-up door illustrates the most common problem business writers have in writing the lead: *they put at the end what should be at the beginning.* How much clearer that report would have been with an opening such as this:

> I recommend replacing the door at the South Loading Warehouse with a heavy-duty, motor-operated roll-up door. The old roll-up door was damaged beyond repair. The opening is now closed with an unsafe temporary wooden structure.

This revision also illustrates that a good lead is not always achieved solely by making sure you don't have at the end what really belongs in the beginning. Important information was also scattered throughout the body that needed to be included in the lead.

Look at these excerpts from a report in which the lead elements were widely scattered throughout the body of the report:

First sentence:	"The following is a summary of the positions we took regarding a request to the IRS for a change in accounting."
Paragraph 2:	"<u>Unbilled revenues</u>: [details] . . . No change in accounting was deemed necessary." [conclusion]
Paragraph 3:	"<u>Bimonthly pilot project</u>: [details] . . . A change in accounting is not necessary." [conclusion]
Paragraph 4:	"<u>Budget billing</u>: [details] . . . We requested a change in accounting." [conclusion]

Paragraph 5:   "New York State Sales Tax: [details] . . . We did not request a change in accounting." [conclusion]

Lead rewrite: Here is a summary of why we asked the IRS for a change in accounting for budget billing and did not request a change for unbilled revenues, the bimonthly pilot project, or New York State Sales Tax.

[Lead summarizes the report's four major conclusions.]

Sometimes a good lead can be a single sentence. For example:

"We had no major problems this month."

This lead is from a monthly progress report on system installation problems. From this, the writer's boss could have assumed that what followed concerned minor problems, and, in fact, he or she might have stopped reading after the first sentence.

Before you can write the lead for your own report, you have to decide what the main points are that you want to make. This may sound obvious and easy, but anyone who has ever done any writing knows that this is probably the most difficult part of writing. Sometimes you don't know what your main points are until you've tried to write a draft. That's why the main points so often do not emerge until the end of the first draft. Part of the redrafting process then involves pulling them up to the beginning.

One good way to practice writing leads is to write them for disorganized reports that either bury the message at the end or scatter it piecemeal throughout the report. This is good training to help you tighten up your own drafts by checking for the most common spots of organizational weakness. With practice, you'll overcome the natural tendency to narrate all of your findings first and become more deft at "starting with the bottom line."

Now you'll have the opportunity to write an improved lead for someone else's report. After that, we'll move on to the second opening strategy: the hook.

Exercise: The Lead

The following is a typical report that could profit from a lead that summarizes its main points. On the worksheet provided, draft a lead that makes the report's purpose clearer. Remember to search for important points that have either been buried at the end or scattered throughout the report.

TO: Divisions A to Z

FROM: John Jones, V.P.

SUBJECT: Items in Short Supply

We are all aware of the energy crisis and the steps being taken by the company to promote its prudent handling. However, less well known are several other items and commodities currently in short supply nationally and projected to remain in short supply for months to come. They include:

A. Paper and paper-related items—Supply very tight and conservatively projected to remain so this year. Many items on allocation by the mills.

B. Lumber—Supply tight, especially pine and hardwood items.

C. Cotton rags—Scarce and becoming more so due to replacement of cotton by synthetic textiles.

D. Steel—Currently on allocation by the mills, with this year's production projected at 5% less than last year's production.

E. Copper—Currently on mill allocation, with deliveries growing more uncertain.

F. Paint—Petrochemical resins and solvents not available as essential paint ingredients, due to concentration of petroleum industry on fuel production.

Traditionally, these items have been so readily available that conservation and restraint were not required. This is no longer the case. The Purchasing Department is making every effort to assure a continued supply. However, it is increasingly important that discipline and planning be employed in their use. The purpose of this memorandum is to highlight these facts and to solicit your attention and assistance.

Your Lead:

Suggested Revision: The Lead

Compare your lead with these suggested revisions. Notice that both of them took most of their content from the *end* of the report. The language has also been made simpler and the sentences are more direct.

Revision 1: We ask your help in conserving the commodities listed below so that the Purchasing Department can continue to supply them. They are in short supply nationwide and will remain so for months.

Revision 2: We must be very conservative in using the following items. They are in short supply nationally and will probably remain scarce for months.

WHETTING THE READER'S APPETITE: THE HOOK

When writers put the bottom-line message toward the end of a report by follow-ing analytical order, they must invite readers to enter into their thinking process or follow trails of evidence with them. This kind of writing requires the involvement of the readers. Involvement implies motivation. Readers need encouragement and other kinds of stimulation to motivate them to follow the writer's path.

Thus when you use this kind of organization, you must "hook" your readers into wanting to read the report. Otherwise, they are likely either not to read it or to skim it superficially. And if you take the trouble to lay out your case before stating an im-portant conclusion or recommendation, you've done so because you want your readers to follow your arguments *carefully*.

Novelists are perhaps the most skilled of all writers at hooking readers. Because a novel may range from a hundred to a thousand pages, readers must be enticed im-mediately to commit themselves. Usually novelists don't want to give away the sto-ry at the beginning, so summarizing the plot is rarely a favored strategy. How, then, do novelists manage to engage their readers in journeys of such epic scope?

Let's take a moment to look at the opening of one of the most successful and fa-mous novels in English: *Tarzan of the Apes* by Edgar Rice Burroughs.

> I heard this story from one who had no business to tell it to me, or to any other. I may credit the seductive influence of an old vintage upon the narrator for the beginning of it, and my own skeptical incredulity during the days that followed for the balance of the strange tale.[1]

From the opening sentence, the writer engages the reader by promising a tale so strange and bizarre that only the "seductive influence of an old vintage" could have wrung it from the narrator. Through a few carefully chosen descriptive phrases— "one who had no business to tell it," "seductive influence," "my own skeptical in-credulity," and "strange tale"—Burroughs piques the reader's interest. The novelist then proceeds to spin out the tale at his chosen pace.

[1] Edgar Rice Burroughs, *Tarzan of the Apes* (New York: Ballentine Books, January, 1976), p. 1.

Similarly, the descriptive power of language coupled with an attempt to involve the reader can transform a pedestrian report opening into one that whets the reader's appetite. For example, look at the opening of a report detailing a number of discrepancies found in an audit the writer reviewed. The report ended with recommendations for establishing a departmental review with auditors before allowing publication of audit reports.

Original opening:

> I reviewed this audit and found a number of discrepancies. We should review reports with our auditors before publication.

It does the job but it's not involving. Now look at a revised version the author came up with.

> When you read how many discrepancies I found when I reviewed this audit, I think you'll agree we should review audit reports with our auditors before publication.

The difference comes from one descriptive phrase, "how many," and taking the time to challenge the readers to find out for themselves whether what the writer says is true. If readers are involved, they are more likely to read a report thoughtfully. In a case like this, in which acceptance of the recommendations at the end hinges on the readers' concurring with the writer's conclusion, it's essential that they be motivated to read the case thoroughly.

Like novelists, you must exercise your creativity to hook your readers. This means thinking about what would be likely to involve them in reading your case. Burroughs knew enough about human psychology to realize that people love an exotic tale, especially if it carries the promise of adventure or danger. Although this technique may not often be available to report writers, there are some standard opening techniques that have been used equally well by creative writers and business writers. Here are some examples.

- Pique the reader's curiosity by posing questions that will be answered in the report.
- Foreshadow the report's findings or conclusions. For example:

  ★ "You will be able to see that ＿＿＿＿＿＿＿＿."

  ★ "You will be a able to see the effect that ＿＿＿＿＿＿ has

  on ＿＿＿＿＿＿."

  ★ "You will be able to understand the impact of ＿＿＿＿＿＿" (some unusual occurrence).

- Engage the reader in an exploration. For example:

  ★ "I've given some thought to _____."

  ★ "I'd like to describe _____."

- Challenge the reader. For example:

  ★ "You will be surprised to find out _____."

  ★ "You would normally expect to see _____ in these circumstances,

    but this report will show that _____" (some unexpected results occurred).

  ★ "This study will show that while _____ might be expected, _____ actually occurred."

One might say that, in the broadest sense, Burroughs' technique is simply a variation on "engaging the reader in an exploration." Whether you're a creative writer or a business writer, you'll have to reach your readers emotionally as well as intellectually if you're going to hook them.

Exercise: Recognizing Effective Hooks

Here are seven examples of openings of business reports in which the writers attempted to hook their readers. As you read them, be aware of their effect on you as a reader. How likely would you be to read the entire report based on the opening sentences? Note your response to each example with a yes or no. Then in the space labeled Why?, explain what appealed to you or what put you off.

1. To determine the best way to teach writing skills to our employees, I conducted a study that asked three questions:

1) Do these people need training?

2) If so, what kind do they need?

3) How can we better manage the development of people's writing skills on an ongoing basis once the training class is over?

I will present my findings and answers to these questions in this report.

Your response: _____

Why? _____

2. A centralized purchasing system has been established whereby Appleby Company can improve the securing of essential materials. This system, once it becomes fully operational, will help us achieve our primary goal of attaining raw materials when needed along with additional auxiliary benefits. This is not presently operational due to the following.

Your response: _____

Why?   _____

3. At the request of John K. Smitherson, I am documenting my conclusions about the problems currently existing with our management development curriculum.

Your response: _____

Why?   _____

4. Your collective response to the questionnaire we recently sent out was unanimous: We must recruit a very special kind of person to lead this department.

Your response: _____

Why?   _____

5. "People learn by doing" is the principle I followed in designing the attached teaching plan.

Your response: _____

Why?   _____

6. The majority of the data required for the first phase of conversion has been received and entered into the databases. The progress of the system has been affected by the trauma of data collection but significant progress continues to be made. During our first efforts at departmental allocations of time-sharing expenditures, a number of observations were made. Some of these have resulted in the following changes designed to facilitate both the feedback process and to provide better information to you.

Your response: _____

Why?   _____

7. Have you ever logged on to your terminal or PC expecting to see your main menu but instead find the message "Reconnected"? Or maybe you hit the enter key and got no response at all?

Your response: _____

Why? _____

COMMENTARY: RECOGNIZING EFFECTIVE HOOKS

Most readers polled in my business writing classes about these examples found 1, 4, 5, and 7 more appealing than 2, 3, and 6. The reasons they gave are the following:

1. Posing questions aroused curiosity and gave readers a sense of the scope and organizational plan of the report.

2. Although the strategy of suggesting a benefit to the new system was potentially appealing, readers were surprised and disappointed to find that the report was actually about why this system was *not* working!

3. The phrase "documenting my conclusions" suggested to most readers something that should be buried in a musty file.

4. The phrase "very special kind of person," although not specific, piqued most people's interest to read on to gain a clearer picture of such a person, especially as their own responses held the key to defining this phrase.

5. The technique of foreshadowing the content of the teaching plan aroused readers' curiosity.

6. The language and sentence structure prevented readers from understanding the message and, therefore, from caring about the value the changes may have had for them.

7. Most readers polled said the questions made them curious to know the answers.

FRONTLOADING AND SIGNING OFF

Whether you elect to summarize your conclusions in a lead paragraph or hook your readers into the report, the intent of these openings is the same: capturing the readers' interest immediately. This principle is often referred to as *frontloading*. In fact, the principle of frontloading underlies most written business communication at every level: the sentence, the paragraph, the overall organization of the report, and the title, which in memoranda takes the form of the *subject title*.

People who first join the business world right out of college or high school are often not very conscious of the principle of frontloading. They are more comfortable with the principle of building up their case slowly in the familiar essay pattern: introduction, body, conclusion. This is the form generally used to explore a thesis. In the academic essay, a proposition or original idea (the thesis) is stated in the introduction, explained, illustrated, or justified in the body, and then reiterated more forcefully at the end.

Even though the pace of introduction and argument may be slower in essays than in reports, essays do observe one important frontloading principle: *the thesis is stated up front.* If you learned to do this in your academic writing classes, you're halfway home to becoming a good business writer.

Thus the form of reports and memoranda is really very similar to the essay. The two major differences are the modifications business writers make in opening and closing a report.

FRONTLOADING TECHNIQUES

As we have discussed, in business writing you will most often state your bottom-line conclusion, recommendation, decision, or judgment in the first paragraph. You do so because the content of most everyday business writing is not controversial or provocative. If you have reason to think an introduction is needed to ease the reader into your bottom-line message, it can be fine-tuned to the readers for whom the report was written.

This kind of introduction—which I term "briefing" and discuss more fully in Chapter 3—is very often combined with a lead or hook into one or more paragraphs. Essays written for a general audience, such as academic essays, often require longer introductions that brief readers on a variety of subjects and issues to prepare them to hear the thesis.

Like essays, reports and memoranda also have **titles** that pinpoint the main message up front. In essays, the title is given first, then the author's name, and then the essay is presented; an essay is, of course, written to anyone who chooses to read it. Reports and memoranda, because they are written to specific people, generally designate who those people are before they specify who the writer is and what the title (or subject) is. They also record the date they were written. As a result, memo headings have four parts:

March 7, 1998

TO: Jay Jones

FROM: Alice Smith

SUBJECT: Evaluation of Program Design

The subject titles of memoranda usually specify the purpose of the report. These are different from the *reference headings* appearing in many letters between the inside address and the salutation. Reference headings refer to previous communications between the reader and writer, such as meetings, telephone conversations, and letters.

Example of Reference Heading

Mr. John Smith

Assistant Director

Property and Casualty Section

Jumbo Life Insurance Company

4 Apple Way

New York, NY 99887

Re: Your letter of August 24, 1998

Dear Mr. Smith:

The best subject titles, just like the titles of essays, should grab the readers' attention and should specify the document's purpose. For example:

Uninformative Subject Title	Informative Subject Title
1. Sure Lure, Inc.	1. Approval of $3MM Line of Credit to Sure Lure, Inc.
2. Progress Report	2. Progress Report on Centralized Purchasing
3. Program Evaluation Findings	3. Findings of Program Evaluation or Why We Need to Hire an Instructional Designer

Often a good subject title will offer a reduced version of the report's main point, as the Sure Lure example illustrates. If the subject title confines itself to the general topic of the report, as in the second example, you must still describe the specific universe of that topic: a progress report *about what?*

The first revision of the third example illustrates a simple frontloading technique: put the key concept—*Findings*—first, not last. The second revision states a reduced version of the report's main recommendation.

Here is how the first revised subject title introduces an opening paragraph:

Subject: <u>Findings of Program Evaluation</u>

I have just completed the first part of the evaluation you requested that I do of our Financial Analysis Preparatory Program. So that I could evaluate the quality of our courses from the student's standpoint, I took three courses our department has been offering for several years: Capital Markets, International Finance, and Corporate Finance. I also took and passed all the exams. The courses, however, were not a totally productive learning experience because their learning objectives were far too broad and ambitious in scope given (1) the entering knowledge of the average learner and (2) the time allotted for each course.

The last sentence states the writer's major conclusion about the program, but the recommendation based on that conclusion was reserved for the end of the report. If the opening paragraph had stated or prepared the reader for the recommendation more specifically than this one does, the more specific subject title would be appropriate. In this case, as the reader will probably be surprised by the recommendation, the writer presents her major conclusion and reasoning before proposing a course of action. Thus she elected the more general subject title.

Here's how the writer might recast her first paragraph to dovetail with the more specific subject title.

Subject: <u>Why We Need to Hire an Instructional Designer</u>

My participation as a student in our Financial Analysis Preparatory Program has led me to some surprising conclusions. The courses we offer now are far too broad and ambitious in scope given (1) the entering knowledge of the average learner and (2) the time allotted for each course. In short, the overall design of the curriculum is flawed, and we should hire an instructional designer to help us redesign the program.

This opening paragraph is more powerful than the other one because the writer leads with her trump card, the recommendation, and summarizes her whole case. Once again, whether you elect your most powerful opening or a slower presentation of the case depends on *your audience*. If, for example, you knew your readers had participated in designing this program you're criticizing, you'd be unwise to tell them up front that their design is flawed and you think a professional needs to clean it up.

Exercise: Clarifying Subject Titles

For the following uninformative subject titles, write informative subject titles that are interesting and that tell the reader *something about the subject* (use your imagination). Or, if appropriate, improve the title by putting the most important word in it up front.

Write a subject title that will help the reader "step into" the opening paragraph.

1. Subject: Pension Plan

2. Subject: Departmental Audit Findings

3. Subject: User ID Location Prefix Proposed Standard

4. Subject: PBX System Automation

5. Subject: Dependent Student Processing

COMMENTARY: CLARIFYING SUBJECT TITLES

Compare your answers with these. These are only samples and other responses are possible.

1. Subject: Benefits of New Pension Plan

2. Subject: Findings of Departmental Audit

3. Subject: Proposal for Standard User ID Code

4. Subject: Automation of PBX System

5. Subject: Processing of Dependent Student Claims

CLOSING A BUSINESS DOCUMENT

A more striking difference between business documents and essays lies in their endings. Closing a report is different from concluding an essay. Essays end with a more powerful statement of the writer's thesis than the one with which he or she began. This added gravity and "conclusiveness" generally come from the writer's desire to leave readers with the most memorable and convincing impression of the thesis possible.

Reports and memoranda, on the other hand, generally close with a statement of the kind of response the writer wants from the readers. They may also close with a course of action the writer wants to propose to the readers.

Here are some examples:

1. We'll need to meet as soon as possible to reach a formal contract agreement by April 1, 1998.

2. I need your decision in writing on this proposal by March 1, 1998, so that we can begin formal negotiations with the customer.

3. Please call me at 832-1102 if you have any questions about following the procedure I've outlined for your employees' use.

4. I am convinced that a professional instructional designer could help us clarify our needs so that we would be able to produce more relevant and successful courses than the ones I attended. Since our boss has been talking about upgrading these courses for a long time, this seems like the right time to give her an action plan to start the ball rolling. Could we set a date sometime next week to put together a full set of recommendations? I'd also like to discuss some other reactions I had to the courses I took."

Closing a report or memorandum should be a good bit simpler than concluding an essay. One thing to avoid, however, is signing off in a formulaic or useless way. This means asking for a response that isn't really a response or trying to say something nice that doesn't actually relate to the document or its purpose.

Here are three examples of formulaic closes:

- I want to thank you in advance for your cooperation. (You're assuming the readers will cooperate—maybe they won't. And you're not specifying what kind of "cooperation" you want.)
- Please let me know your decision at your earliest convenience. (If you give readers this kind of leeway, they may feel no urgency to get back to you—ever!)
- Thank you for your attention. (Again, you're not being specific enough about the kind of response you want from the readers. This is like thanking them for reading the document.)

If you're not recommending action or you don't really want a response from readers other than for them to read the report or memo, *stop* at the end. You don't have to repeat your main points or thank them for reading your writing. If your organization was clear and your writing readable, readers should have found the report an informative and, at the very least, painless experience.

Exercise: Closing Business Documents

Below are six examples of endings of business reports, letters, and memoranda. Note in the spaces provided whether you think they are "appropriate" or "inappropriate" closings. If they are inappropriate closings, describe why you think they are inappropriate in the space provided.

1. Your prompt attention in this matter would be greatly appreciated.

[ ] appropriate

[ ] inappropriate

If inappropriate, why?

2. I think you will see in the memo that I have brought attention to some valuable information.

   [ ] appropriate

   [ ] inappropriate

If inappropriate, why?

3. Information on these companies should be sent to reach me no later than MON-DAY, MAY 6. If you feel you will have difficulty meeting this deadline, please let me know as soon as possible.

   [ ] appropriate

   [ ] inappropriate

If inappropriate, why?

4. We would appreciate your earliest attention to this matter to provide for the time-ly division of responsibilities and the initiation of planning and testing by the re-spective auditing groups. We are available to discuss this letter with you at your convenience. Please contact me with any questions or comments.

   [ ] appropriate

   [ ] inappropriate

If inappropriate, why?

5. Participants were given the survey and will complete it before our meeting on Friday, Oct. 3. I will then forward all surveys to Ed Andrews so that he can tabulate the results. If you need any additional information, please call me at extension 5500.

[ ] appropriate

[ ] inappropriate

If inappropriate, why?

6. I know that you're pretty busy, but for the sake of double-checking in the future, I would be most appreciative to get a written response to most of these questions.

[ ] appropriate

[ ] inappropriate

If inappropriate, why?

COMMENTARY: CLOSING BUSINESS DOCUMENTS

1. [X] inappropriate

The closing does not state what kind of action the writer wants the reader to take. "Attention" is a mental activity, not an action.

2. [X] inappropriate

The writer appears to "pat himself on the back" about what he has said in the memo. The reader should be free to decide how effectively or ineffectively the writer makes his point. Also, the writer does not state an action he wants the reader to take or an action he plans to take.

3. [X] appropriate

The writer clearly tells readers what he or she wants them to do in response to the memo.

4. [X] inappropriate

The ending needs to state specifically when the writer needs a response and exactly what kind of response he or she expects. The writer should avoid vague phrasing such as "your earliest attention," "timely," and "at your convenience."

5. [X] appropriate

The writer tells the reader a specific action she will take. She also states what will happen as a result of her actions. She encourages phone calls by providing her direct extension.

6. [X] inappropriate

The writer does not specify which questions he or she wants the reader to answer. If left to their own devices, readers may choose (inadvertently or on purpose) to answer the wrong questions.

A WORD ABOUT E-MAIL

E-mail is, by design, a frontloaded form of communication. Originally conceived as short, single-screen messages, the e-mail format takes all of the informational elements of reports and letters, including the cc (copied) readers and bcc (blind-copied) readers normally shown at the end of documents, and pushes them to the front.

> To:
> From:
> Subject:
> Cc:
> Bcc:
> X-Attachments:

As a result of its frontloaded layout, readers expect the subject title to tell them most of what they need to learn from the e-mail, along with the first sentence. Readers also assume that writers use e-mail when it is a better way of communicating with them than a phone call, voice mail, or paper report.

In reality, of course, e-mail can fall prey to the same bad writing habits as paper writing. The message may lack the frontloaded title, statement of purpose in the first paragraph, and action statements of who needs to do what, just as paper documents do. In addition, some writers fill the single screen with unformatted prose or write messages that encompass many screens. Such messages have to be printed out for easy readability, thereby defeating the original intent of e-mail as a fast-reading electronic communication. All the writer gains in such cases is the ability to transmit a long document more quickly.

People who use e-mail frequently generally agree on a few rules of etiquette and style that help the medium work best.

EFFECTIVE E-MAIL MESSAGES

* Specify purpose up front in subject title, first sentence, or first paragraph.
* Respect the reader's time. Considerate e-mail writers avoid broadcasting messages to people who will not know why they are receiving them.
* Attach long documents. The e-mail itself serves as a cover note telling readers the purpose of the attached documents and why they are receiving them.
* Compose messages in concise, clear language.
* State what actions, if any, readers should take in response to the e-mail.

In short, if you observe the same principles we discussed in the previous section—frontloading your purpose and specifying actions readers should take—you will write e-mails that communicate clearly and effectively.

INDUCTIVE VERSUS DEDUCTIVE LOGIC

No book on writing is complete without looking at the subject of logic, for logic is the foundation of organization. You already know a lot more about it than you may realize.

Logic is defined by one authority as "the study of the strength of the evidential link between the premises and conclusions of arguments."[2] Academic logicians fashion these links with relentless intellectual precision. In everyday business life, one must also take care that the evidence and reasoning underlying decisions are strong and valid. If decisions are not reasonable given the facts of a situation, the actions taken on the basis of them are not likely to yield useful or profitable results.

[2]Brian Skyrms, *Choice and Chance: An Introduction to Inductive Logic.* Third Edition (Belmont, CA: Wadsworth, 1986), p. 4.

Because logic is such a precise subject, there are many misconceptions about it. One of the most common is what makes an argument deductive or inductive.

> One of the most widespread misconceptions of logic is the belief that deductive arguments proceed from the general to the specific, and inductive arguments proceed from the specific to the general. Such a view is nonsense, for . . . arguments do not fall into two categories: deductive and inductive. . . . the difference between inductively strong and deductively valid arguments is not to be found in the generality or particularity of premises and conclusion but rather in the definitions of deductive validity and inductive strength.[3]

This passage discusses a couple of important points about induction and deduction that are useful for everyday business thinkers and writers to consider. First, the "widespread misconception" the writer refers to has nevertheless been of some use in helping people think about organizing their thoughts on paper. (Thus you'll see some textbooks refer to "most important to least important" organization as "deductive" organization.) The important point, however, is that the true strength of any argument lies in *how valid it really is*. Validity comes from the truth of the evidence presented and the reasonableness of the links between evidence and conclusions.

The mark of a true deductive argument is that the conclusion *must* be true if the premises are true. The classic deductive argument is the syllogism:

> All men are mortal.
>
> Aristotle is a man.
>
> Therefore, Aristotle is mortal.

Syllogisms embody the same reasoning process you followed when you did proofs in geometry class. Geometry proofs start with a principle or axiom the truth of which is absolute. You reason from this axiom through a series of interlocking steps, each of which necessarily follows from the previous step. If your logic is sound and you've not skipped a step, your conclusion is proved and must be valid.

Inductive logic is more creative than deductive logic. In an inductive argument, the conclusion goes beyond the factual claims of the premise. For example:

— Four women carrying bouquets and wearing long dresses were seen entering the church.

— Four men wearing tuxedos and boutonnieres were seen entering the church.

— The minister was seen entering the church.

Therefore, it is likely that a wedding is about to take place in the church.

[3]Skyrms, pp. 13, 15.

As our logic authority puts it, "an inductively strong argument risks more than a deductively valid one; it risks the possibility of leading from true premises to a false conclusion."[4] In this example, all of the people observed might have been attending a ball being held in the church, although this conclusion does not seem as probable as the other conclusion.

The end point of an inductive argument is the discovery of a new fact or insight. The ability to create a theory or conceptualize a new idea is a creative act of induction. Scientists, conceptualizers, and philosophers pray for this moment to happen to them as they pursue their studies in their chosen disciplines. Yet no one really knows where this marvelous ability comes from.

Happily, we all have the ability to gain insight or conceptualize new ideas to a greater or lesser extent. It happens when, after studying a difficult subject for a long time, you finally understand a concept or grasp the meaning of something.

Business writing, like all other writing, is only as good as the thinking that underlies it. And business people, like scientists, logicians, or anyone who purports to reach conclusions on the basis of a logical process, will intuitively use inductive and deductive logic. Their writing will contain statements of "insights" or conclusions, supported by a logic that proves the validity or, at least, acceptability of those insights.

Given the nature of these two reasoning processes and the conclusions they produce, you'll find that most everyday arguments, if analyzed, are inductive rather than deductive. Most real-life situations cannot be made to conform easily to the rigors of deductive logic. As you can imagine, arguments presented in strict syllogistic form, though airtight, are necessarily repetitious and sometimes pedantic. A paragraph might lend itself to this pattern more easily than a whole report, and it is at the level of presenting evidence that you'll sometimes see a true deductive argument. Because inductive arguments allow the writer a greater measure of creativity and opportunities for discovery, the overall logic of a report is usually inductive.

If we think of the organization of business writing in terms of a continuum, then we'd have to say that the two extremes of organization are pure deductive argumentation and merely stating an opinion without any supporting evidence. Business writing will generally fall somewhere between these two extremes.

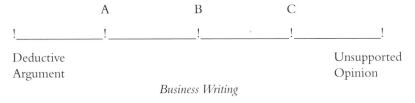

	A	B	C	
Deductive Argument				Unsupported Opinion

Business Writing

[4]Skyrms, p. 8.

As a writer you must choose your point on this continuum for each communication.

For example, if you place yourself at point C, near the extreme of unsupported opinion, you'll probably choose a method of organization such as most important to least important order. That is, you will probably state your opinion, decision, conclusion, or recommendation first, and then the reasoning supporting your position. That reasoning could be inductive, deductive, or a combination of the two, but the emphasis of the report is clearly on *your position*.

If you wish to be at point A, your emphasis will be on organizing a logical journey for the readers to help them enter into your thinking process so that they will be more likely to agree with your position. The report will emphasize the *importance of the logic of your process* as much as the conclusion or result of your logic. You're inviting readers to observe your thought process and judge the results of it independently. Again, your logic could be deductive, inductive, or a combination of the two.

If you wish to be at point B on the continuum, then you'd probably use a logical journey as a basic organizing strategy, but maybe you'd take more shortcuts and require more intellectual leaps from your readers in following your logic than you did at point A. By providing readers with a less-detailed roadmap of your thinking, you assume that they need less explanation, persuading, or "hand-holding" to understand your message than your readers at point A.

Once again, it's thinking about the readers and determining what *they need or want to know* that forms the basis of your organization plan. There are as many points on this continuum as there are different kinds of readers.

On the next page, you'll read some business reports that argue inductively. Three types of possible readers are described for each report. In the spaces provided, decide which reader would find the report most persuasive and note *why* you think so.

Exercise: Logic and Argumentation

You're going to have the opportunity to read three business reports that attempt to persuade through logical argument. You'll then be asked to decide which of the following readers would find the report most persuasive.

1. A reader who already has knowledge of the case being presented and is especially interested in *your position*. On our continuum of report organization, this is the reader at point C—the reader nearest the extreme of "unsupported opinion."

2. A reader who has very little knowledge of the case being presented and who needs a thorough explanation of facts and reasoning to be persuaded. On our con-

tinuum, this is the reader near point A—the reader who needs to be invited to enter your thinking process to be persuaded of your conclusions.

3. A reader who may have some knowledge of the case being presented, but who will still require considerable explanation to be persuaded. This is the reader near point B on our continuum—the reader with whom you might take more logical shortcuts than the reader at point A.

Here's the continuum. Refer back to page 36 for explanations of its points.

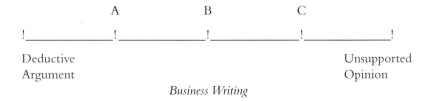

A   B   C

!_____!_____!_____!_____!

Deductive   Unsupported
Argument   Opinion

Business Writing

Report No. 1

Subject: *Progress Report on Centralized Purchasing*

As you are aware, a letter was released from this office regarding our new corporate policy of reporting all purchase contracts in excess of $10,000. To date, we have received no response from the manufacturing facilities. There are a number of possible explanations for this with varying implications.

First, it is possible that $10,000 was an inappropriate level in that most contracts negotiated were under this level. An appropriate response to this problem would be to reassess historic purchasing levels in order to establish an appropriate threshold.

Second, the problem may have resulted from the fact that the letter was released on a date too close to the peak buying season, thus not allowing the respective executives adequate time to assimilate the request into their current purchasing procedures. Should this be the case, we should begin to realize the expected benefits of the new directive when the next buying cycle begins.

Third, the problem may represent a message from the purchasing executives that they resent head office tampering with their established routines. In this event, we would need to make them realize the benefits that everyone will gain if they comply with this procedure.

In my opinion, the first explanation is most likely. An appropriate course of action at this point would be to arrange a conference of all the purchasing executives to discuss the problem as a group. Such a conference would also allow us to talk to each executive.

This memo would be most persuasive to:

Reader #1, at point C on the continuum _____

Reader #2, at point A on the continuum _____

Reader #3, at point B on the continuum _____

Why?_____

Report No. 2

Subject: *Approval of $3MM Line of Credit to Russ Yelverton, Inc.*

Introduction: The requested line would be used to purchase putty and cleaning solvents to give the company twelve months' worth of supplies. Volume discounts are important to Yelverton's cost control and will continue its competitive advantage. The low-budget car- painting business is subject to increasing competition. Yelverton is protecting its market share through cost-effective measures such as volume discounts.

Credit Considerations: Yelverton's conservative balance sheet and low interest expense point to a large debt capacity. Leverage ratios are low because the company has very little debt. Debt is supported by high owner's equity of 69.6%.

Management is protecting its market niche with cost controls and expansion into new markets. Management has plans to add 25 shops in the United States this year and has already opened three new shops in London. Industry trends are favorable because consumers are keeping old cars longer. As the market leader and founder of the quick and easy paint job, Yelverton is dedicated to its primary business.

Cost controls and expanded markets mark Yelverton's corporate philosophy. Cost of goods sold to sales was up to 88.5% in 1998 from 85.2% in 1997. The purchase of volume discounts will help Yelverton cut costs and thus preserve its market niche of "no frills paint jobs."

Recommendation: Approval of the $3MM line is requested.

This memo would be most persuasive to:

Reader #1, at point C on the continuum _____

Reader #2, at point A on the continuum _____

Reader #3, at point B on the continuum _____

Why?_____

Report No. 3

Subject: *Findings of Program Evaluation*

I have just completed the first part of the evaluation you requested that I do of our Financial Analysis Preparatory Program. So that I could evaluate the quality of our courses from the student's standpoint, I took three courses our department has been offering for several years: Capital Markets, International Finance, and Corporate Finance. I also took and passed all of the exams. The courses, however, were not a totally productive learning experience because their learning objectives were far too broad and ambitious in scope given (1) the entering knowledge of the average learner and (2) the time allotted for each course.

You may be surprised to find out that these courses are each only two days long yet purport to teach recent historical developments, the most important theoretical developments, and a fairly generous sampling of some important technical tools common to each subject. The average student is a recent college graduate with a B.A. in business or a general liberal arts degree. The material was new to most of them. As a result, they focused their attention on taking copious notes and "cramming" for the final exam. After the exam, the information was promptly forgotten—at least, that was my experience and the experience of at least twenty other students I spoke to.

For these courses to result in successful retention of learning, they should be redesigned and, in my opinion, should also be made much more narrow in scope. We cannot hope to provide students with either a broad or deep acquaintance with these subjects in a few days. And the question is—do we even want to try? For example, some knowledge must be memorized, but some can be looked up when needed.

One may only need to know where and how to locate the information. As the courses are currently taught, however, we require memorization of a wide range of assorted facts and principles, most of which bear little relevance to anything the student will immediately do.

If a proper assessment of the needs inherent in these courses were done, it would then be possible for our staff to design the curriculum and teaching strategies that would really meet those needs. I am convinced that a professional instructional designer could help us clarify our needs so that we would be able to produce more relevant and successful courses than the ones I attended. Since our boss has been talking about upgrading these courses for a long time, this seems like the right time to give her an action plan to start the ball rolling. Could we set a date sometime next week to put together a full set of recommendations? I'd also like to discuss some other reactions I had to the courses I took.

This memo would be most persuasive to:

Reader #1, at point C on the continuum ＿＿＿＿＿＿

Reader #2, at point A on the continuum ＿＿＿＿＿＿

Reader #3, at point B on the continuum ＿＿＿＿＿＿

Why?＿＿＿＿＿＿＿＿＿＿＿＿＿＿＿＿＿＿＿＿＿＿＿＿＿

COMMENTARY: LOGIC AND ARGUMENTATION

1. Report 1 would probably be most persuasive to reader #1, the reader near point C who is primarily interested in the writer's position. Although the writer presents some indication of his reasoning process, the evidence that caused him to prefer one of the positions he presents over the others is not stated. Thus the final conclusion of the report is little more than an unsupported opinion.

This kind of strategy is risky at best. Probably only a couple of sentences would be needed to explain the opinion stated in the last paragraph. Unless the reader is the writer's good buddy, he or she is likely to feel annoyed by the omission of any explanation for the final conclusion.

2. Report 2 would probably be most persuasive to reader #3, the reader near point B on the continuum. The writer presents some evidence and reasoning for the decision, but the argument rests to a large degree on thinly supported assertions. Here are some examples:

> A. "The low-budget car-painting business is subject to increasing competition. Yelverton is protecting its market share through cost-effective measures such as volume discounts."

> *Comment on logic:* What's the relationship between cutting costs and staving off the competition?

> B. "As the market leader and founder of the quick and easy paint job, Yelverton is dedicated to its primary business."

> *Comment on logic:* Even though a company has invented a product and is the leading seller of the product, these facts alone do not ensure that the company will continue to dedicate itself to producing and selling this product as its primary business. Indeed, the whole paragraph that this sentence comes from has no logic unless the reader already knows a lot more about the company and its strategies than the writing presents.

> C. "The purchase of volume discounts will help Yelverton cut cost costs and thus preserve its market niche of 'no frills paint jobs.'"

> *Comment on logic:* This is the same assertion we discussed in point A: how will cutting costs help stave off the competition and preserve the company's market niche? The report makes this point over and over again (talk about belaboring!) but never explains the reasoning behind the conclusion.

The writer assumes the reader knows that in the low-cost car-painting industry, the market leader has traditionally been the vendor who can offer the lowest prices. One way to keep prices down is to keep costs down. Thus any cost savings resulting from this purchase can be passed along to the customers.

If the reader is well acquainted with this company, its competition, and the industry in which it operates, he or she can color in a lot of the evidential links that are missing from this report. For anyone else, the report is little more than a loosely assembled string of unsupported assertions, some of which are repeated several different ways in lieu of real evidence. In some ways, this report is closer to the realm of unsupported opinion than the first example, although the report emphasizes argumentation over the writer's opinion.

3. Report 3 would probably be most persuasive to reader #2, the reader near point A on the continuum. The report works through considerable explanation and ev-

idence before presenting its final recommendation that they should hire an instructional designer.

The ending also indicates that the writer probably had a lot of other arguments and evidence to present in support of her case, but elected to present only the main one in the report. This is a good strategy if your readers, like many busy professionals, prefer to read reports that are as short as possible. Some executives refuse ever to read more than a one-page report. Sometimes a report must serve as the hook for a fuller discussion of the case in some other forum.

CHAPTER 3

Developing the Document's Structure

Introductory Techniques: Briefing
The Paragraph
Transitions
Emotional Arguments: The Art of Persuasion

INTRODUCTORY TECHNIQUES: BRIEFING

Sometimes the reader needs to be given background information or be apprised of a special situation giving rise to a particular business document. I call this kind of introduction *briefing* in the sense of giving precise instructions or essential information. You might also think of this as a customized introduction that prepares your particular readers to hear your message.

You're already familiar with the process of briefing whether you know it or not. When you invite your in-laws for dinner, you might brief them about the arrival time, whether the children will be there to greet them, what you're planning to serve, or how many other guests were invited. Commentators on the evening news often report that the president's press secretary met with him to "brief" him before a news conference. This means the press secretary armed him with vital facts, statistics, and other information to use in fielding reporters' questions.

You might reasonably ask, why can't a business document simply begin "I've decided," "I've concluded," or "I recommend?" Why not just start with the lead or hooking paragraph, the way newspaper writers do?

You *can* in some cases and *not* in other. The briefing *prepares the reader to understand your purpose for having written the document.* That is, if readers are not familiar with the situation that gave rise to the document, you may have to take time to brief them on the necessary background. If they have the background, the briefing may be no more than a simple phrase to remind them of the occasion, such as, "As you re-quested" or "In light of . . . " (followed by a brief statement of the situation prompt-ing the document).

If you know the reader knows why the document is being written and he or she is a very informal, "get-to-the point" sort of person, you can simply begin "I recom-mend" or "I've decided" and dispense with briefing.

Here is an example of a memorandum seeking approval of a customer's request for a loan. It was written by a junior credit officer to an approving credit officer sever-al steps above him in the approval hierarchy. Here's how the memo would open *without briefing:*

TO: Approving Officer

FROM: Junior Credit Officer

SUBJECT: *Approval of $200M Line of Credit to Sure Lure Company*

I recommend we extend the $200M line of credit to Sure Lure Company with the following restriction:

- Under a borrowing base formula, lend 90% against receivables that are current or no more than 90 days past due.

The restriction protects the bank from the line being used to

- Support unsold inventory, or
- Finance poor quality receivables.

If the officer knows the company and what it intends to use the loan to finance, he or she might appreciate such a direct opening.

However, as often happens in large organizations, if the approving officer does not know the customer or the purpose of the loan, this opening may seem presumptu-ous. "How am I supposed to know what this is all about?" might be the reaction. In such a case, the reader would expect to be *prepared* to understand the recom-mendation. Even though the body of the report would undoubtedly explain the reasons for the decision, the opening might put the reader in an unreceptive frame of mind to hear the writer's argument.

Thus before you write a briefing, you must consider:

- *Who* the readers are
- *Why* they need background
- *What* information they need to know

Once you've answered the questions *who, what,* and *why,* you should have a good sense of what information you need to give the reader. Be careful that you do not present a lot of facts that may be interesting but do not really help prepare readers for the case explained in the document. Nothing is more aggravating than a report that starts off with a turgidly written lump of ill-digested or poorly organized facts and statistics. The readers' first impulse will probably be to trash it. Remember: first impressions count in writing too. If one part of the report has to be exquisitely well written, it is the briefing. Edit, rewrite, and edit again until you've made it a polished gem.

Briefings generally take one of two forms. One is a cover memo that prepares the reader for something it's attached to. Here's an example:

TO: Managers

FROM: Joe Jones, System Consultant

SUBJECT: First Aid Kit

Have you ever logged on to your terminal or PC expecting to see your LOFS main menu but instead find the message "Reconnected"? Or maybe you hit the enter key and got no response at all? Well, the answers to these and other perplexing systems quirks are being addressed in a VM First Aid Kit. The attached kit contains a list of frequent problems and their solutions for both the PC and the terminal.

A LOFS reference card will also be available in September. It will contain some helpful information and instructions on using LOFS major functions.

If you have any questions about the First Aid Kit, call Jane or Kate in the Info Center on extension 7790 or 7650.

Cover memos are often used to introduce an attachment or summarize the findings of a longer research report.

A second common form of briefing is an introductory paragraph or paragraphs that prepare the readers for the report to come. Here's the lead excerpt you saw earlier preceded by briefing:

TO: Approving Officer

FROM: Junior Credit Officer

SUBJECT: *Approval of $200M Line of Credit to Sure Lure Company*

Sure Lure is an old, family-run fishing lure manufacturing company. The company increased its sales in 1998 by 16% to $9,717,940, placing it tenth among the top ten lure manufacturers. Recent plant modernization is likely to keep the company among the leaders in this steadily growing and highly competitive industry, which supplies the third most popular participation sport in the U.S.

The company plans to use the requested line of credit to enter the retail market. This is a new market for Sure Lure, which has always sold to regional wholesalers. This line would allow the company to

- Increase stock in anticipation of new sales, and
- Extend credit to new retail customers.

I recommend that we extend the $200M line of credit to Sure Lure with the following restriction:

- Under a borrowing base formula, lend 90% against receivables that are current or no more than 90 days past due.

The restriction protects the bank from the line being used to

- Support unsold inventory, or
- Finance poor quality receivables.

Notice that the writer has been very selective about what information is presented in the briefing. Without going into a lot of detail, he selects a few key facts to paint the picture of a moderately successful company (tenth among the top ten) in a promising industry ("steadily growing and highly competitive"). A key adverb within a judgmental statement should predispose the reader to view a fact about the company as a predictor of future success: "Recent plant modernization [fact] is *likely* [adverb] to *keep the company among the leaders*" [judgment]. He also briefs the reader about the purpose for which the loan was requested—one of the first things any credit officer wants to know. Clearly, he knows the type of person he's writing for, even though he may not know the individual personally.

Once again, the key to writing effective briefings is thinking about the readers, their attitudes, their knowledge, and their needs. In business writing, you often know the person or persons you're writing to personally. Even if you don't know them personally, as might be the case of the junior credit officer writing to someone higher up in the approval chain, you'll probably know who they are and what they would expect to see in your report simply by virtue of their job or function in the company. You can "fine-tune" your briefing and arguments accordingly.

Exercise: Briefing

Read the following briefing paragraph:

> This memorandum marks the official beginning of the 1998 Planning and Budgeting Process for the department. As many of you have heard, our approach this year will be significantly different from previous years. Each area will be asked to use a new procedure to plan and write its budget report. This memo will explain the steps of the new procedure and how to document them.

This briefing appears to be written for readers who have heard that a new procedure is coming. Nothing in the writing indicates that the writer expects any resistance from the readers toward the procedure or the contents of the report.

Now read the following descriptions of two different types of readers who are going to receive this memorandum. Then rewrite the paragraph above for *each* of the different audiences. Use language and explanations that will influence them to be receptive to the report. Assume that the basic information contained in the paragraph above will be sufficient for each of these audiences. The descriptions will provide you with any other information you might need.

Briefing Situation #1

You are writing to a group of managers who are not aware that the Central Comptroller's Area wants them to use a new procedure for the 1998 Planning and Budgeting Process. They are likely to be unpleasantly surprised by the new requirement. They may think this method is unnecessarily detailed and will make preparation of the budget more difficult than it needs to be. You'll have to emphasize that because company expenses and staff levels have been rising significantly over the last three years, a more precise budget plan is needed from each department so that the Central Comptroller's Area can track all company expenses more closely. The procedure will also enable each department to get a much clearer picture of its expenses than it has had in the past.

Your Revision:

Briefing Situation #2

You are writing to a group of managers who actually participated in helping you prepare the new procedure that must be used to submit their 1998 budgets. Several managers consulted with you about the problems creating the need for a new procedure before you wrote it. Several other managers read drafts of the procedure that you submitted to them and gave you many useful suggestions for ways to improve and simplify it. As a result, you were able to draft a procedure that is clearly written and will be easy to use.

Your Revision:

COMMENTARY: BRIEFING

Once again, inasmuch as I can't give you direct commentary on your writing, I'm providing sample revisions with analytical commentary on the language and techniques used to influence the readers. I again suggest that you show your work to a friend, asking him or her to respond in light of the principles discussed in the lesson.

Sample Revision: Briefing Situation #1

We all know that company expenses and staff levels have been rising significantly over the last three years. As a result, the Central Comptroller's Area has asked each department to provide them with more precise budget plans this year so that they will be able to track overall company expenses more closely. This report will explain exactly how to use the new procedure for preparing your budget that the Comptroller's Area has developed. You'll find that the details they're asking you to provide will help you watch your area's expenses more closely, thus benefiting your department as well as the company in general.

Comment

The briefing begins by reminding readers of a noncontroversial fact that they all know and will agree with. The writer then explains how this fact has caused the comptrollers to need more precise information in the budgets than they've needed in the past. The writer emphasizes the *causes* leading to the new procedure rather than the effect, the procedure itself. A key adverb, *exactly,* suggests that the report will give them precise instructions for using the procedure, which should assuage some fears they may have about having to do the budgets a different way. The briefing closes by emphasizing that the departments will benefit from the change as well as the company in general—a strategy that should further motivate the readers to want to use the procedure.

Sample Revision: Briefing Situation #2

Once again, I'd like to thank each of you for your many helpful suggestions about the best way to standardize the new budget procedure for all the departments. I think you'll find that the procedure explained below is clear and easy to use, primarily because of your editing and ideas for ways to improve and simplify it.

Comment

A "thank you" and a pat on the back for a job well done are always appreciated, yet these simple gestures of common courtesy are too often neglected in the business world. The paragraph also centers on the contribution the readers made to the procedure, not the work the memo writer did in writing the actual procedure. This strategy, which is often called "you-centered" writing as opposed to "I-centered" writing, is almost always a sure motivator and is a favorite strategy of salesmen and sales writers. Let's face it, everyone responds to a compliment, especially if it is sincere and deserved.

THE PARAGRAPH

Paragraphs are the building blocks business writers use to build the report's structure. Reports, like buildings, can only be solid edifices if the overall plan is architecturally sound, the blocks themselves are well made, and the mortar that holds them together is firm.

A report is like a well-made building in that the sequence of the paragraphs reflects the author's logic, the transitions help the reader follow the logic the argument is built on, and the paragraphs themselves explain the main points of the argument. Let's look now at reports from the smallest structural component outward: *Paragraph Development, Paragraph Sequencing,* and *Transitions.*

PARAGRAPH DEVELOPMENT

Once you've hooked your readers' interest or summarized your main points in the lead, you've got to decide how to explain your thinking in the rest of the report. Clearly, the first paragraph cannot tell the whole story. The body of the report must supply the details and arguments the readers need to comprehend your thinking fully.

Several kinds of thought processes yield ways to organize paragraphs. The most common ones are:

1. *Cause and effect analysis,* which means explaining why an event had a certain result or how a certain result stemmed from a particular event.
2. *Comparison and contrast,* which means comparing a group of similarities, a group of differences, or a combination of the two in explaining a general point.
3. *Giving examples,* which is the way you *illustrate* a general point with concrete examples.

These ways of organizing thoughts into paragraphs arise easily and nonmechanically as you think and write. No one consciously says to himself, "I am now going to organize this paragraph by using comparison and contrast." Rather, as someone explains what he thinks—say, in the case of approving a customer's request for a personal loan—he may decide to point out that the customer has $10,000 more in her savings account in 1998 than she did in 1997. He naturally *contrasts* these two figures to show that the customer's savings have increased. Then from there he might want to go further, based on the evidence, to argue that the customer's increased savings indicate an improvement in her overall financial position *because* of something else the banker knows about her. Now he's using cause and effect analysis. And, of course, the original example of $10,000 is an illustration as well as a comparison.

Cause and effect analysis involves questioning the *reasons* that something happened and is often used in problem solving. If you ask the question, Why did this happen? your answer will be the causes. If your question is, What will this result in? your answer will be the effects. When you say, "The company is losing money because of poor cost controls, high salaries, and incompetent management," you are dealing with cause. When you say, "The company's poor cost controls, high salaries, and incompetent management will probably make it go bankrupt," you are dealing with effect. Cause explains the past, whereas effect predicts the future.

Comparison means analyzing the ways in which two things are alike, and contrast is analyzing the ways they are unalike. As a developmental technique, comparisons or contrasts can be isolated examples in a paragraph or large-scale organizing strategies.

The first and most important step of any comparison or contrast is deciding on the points to be compared or contrasted. For example, let's say you want to develop the idea that a good manager of people can easily be distinguished from a bad manager of people. To do this, you would ask yourself in what areas you do want to contrast the activities of bad managers with good managers. Let's say you choose three points of contrast: (1) time spent on counseling, (2) division of workload, (3) willingness to praise. A simple and useful outline would be three parallel columns:

	Good managers	Bad managers
1. Time spent on counseling	Manager keeps an open-door policy and encourages dialogue with subordinates.	Manager is inaccessible or tends to hide in his office. Questions are ignored or evaded.
2. Division of workload	Manager divides workload fairly among subordinates and according to their talents.	Manager shows favoritism, giving the best assignments to personal favorites.
3. Willingness to praise	Manager gives frequent encouragement and suggests ways to improve.	Manager never gives a compliment but is quick to criticize.

After you've done your outline, you turn it into prose by adding the transitional words and phrases that will help the reader follow the points of the contrast. The transitional words and sentences have been underlined.

> After working in an office for a while, most people can easily distinguish a good manager of people from a bad manager of people. One immediately noticeable characteristic of good managers is their "open-door" policy. Employees know they can, in most cases,

drop by without an appointment to discuss a problem or ask a question. Bad managers, <u>on the other hand</u>, shy away from dialogue and hide in their offices with the door closed. Even making an appointment does not ensure a conference, for the employee is often bumped for "more important meetings" or sudden changes in the boss's schedule.

<u>Another clear-cut difference between good and bad managers is the way they assign work</u>. The good manager gives considerable thought to employees' skills, talents, and interests before giving out projects. Sometimes a task that will be difficult is assigned to develop an employee's area of weakness, but the major criterion is always which employee can do the job most successfully. Bad managers, <u>however</u>, tend to give the plum assignments to their favorites, even if someone else could do them better. Work is therefore divided politically, according to the managers' personal likes and dislikes. They rarely consider who would be the best person for the job.

<u>Good and bad managers differ markedly in their willingness to give a compliment</u>. Good managers are glad to give credit where credit is due, and often praise good work. When they see an area in which an employee can improve, they offer specific, but sensitive suggestions. <u>On the contrary</u>, bad managers are quick to criticize, but rarely, if ever, give compliments. In fact, personal comments to employees of any kind are terse and few.

When analyzing through comparison or contrast, keep in mind that you must give equal attention to *both* sides. Otherwise, your analysis will be slanted.

Illustration of points is one of the simplest and most natural ways writers explain themselves. A good example is often remembered long after the point it illustrated is forgotten. Examples also often capture the attention and interest of the reader in hearing a point before it is actually stated.

Recently, I met a commercial banker who told me the following: "You know, not too long ago, all that a commercial banker had to do to generate business was to handle a knife and fork and play golf." That was in the era when banks were regulated and competitors were few. Today, bankers play an entirely different game.

The example quoted at the beginning is striking, a little funny, and likely to "hook" the reader into the paragraph. Examples provide detail, color, and liveliness in writing. Without them, the reader is never really sure of exactly what the writer thinks, for the writing lacks specificity. A writer should not expect the reader to color in the examples illustrating his or her points.

Writers need to be able to recognize the ways these thought processes manifest themselves in writing, not so that they will elect to use any one in particular but so that they can elect to *use them all* and naturally weave them together.

One way to become clearer about how to let these processes happen is to recognize when they have been used by other people in their writing. In a moment, you'll have the opportunity to identify these thought processes "in action."

Exercise: Paragraph Development

Read the following paragraphs. You'll notice that certain sections of sentences have been numbered. In the spaces provided after each paragraph, which are numbered to correlate with the underlined parts of the paragraph, identify whether the underlined section shows a use of cause and effect analysis, comparison, contrast, or illustration.

Paragraph One

We have known for some time that (1) <u>since the profit economics of commercial banking have changed, traditional credit products are no longer sufficient</u> to meet the wide range of credit and noncredit financing options available to the largest corporations. Hence, (2) <u>the predominant lending focus of the commercial banker has given way</u> to a more broad-based financial marketing role. (3) <u>Metro Bank, through the unique strengths of its relationship marketing and management approach, may have a competitive advantage</u> in the race among banks to reposition themselves in the marketplace.

Example 1: _____

Example 2: _____

Example 3: _____

Paragraph Two

Effective January 1, 1987, the Tax Reform Act of 1986 will alter the tax treatment of meals and entertainment expenses. (1) <u>Under the prior law, these expenses were 100% deductible</u> when proven to be directly related to the active conduct of Bufoe Corporation's business. (2) <u>However, under the Tax Reform Act of 1986, business-related meal and entertainment expenses are only 80% deductible</u> with some exceptions.

Example 1: _____

Example 2: _____

Paragraph Three

At present, no standard of taste has been endorsed by management for the Executive Summary's organization. In fact, the general policy has been to encourage employees to avoid using a model for the summary and instead to exercise "creativity" in constructing their format. At the same time, however, (1) <u>some managers have informally circulated a memo dated May 1, 1998, for employees to use as a model</u>. Because each case is unique, the same format will not apply to every report. (2) <u>Thus when employees attempt to apply the model format to their writing, they usually have problems.</u>

Example 1: _____

Example 2: _____

Paragraph Four

Cranford Corporation continued to repay long-term debt and short term borrowings. (1) <u>Trade payables increased slightly in line with receivables</u>. Liquidity was generally maintained. (2) <u>Cash flow from earnings, conversion of debentures into equity, and a reduction in working investment have enabled Cranford Corporation to reduce leverage to the lowest level of any of the major trading companies</u>. Subsidiaries are also generally well capitalized, and (3) <u>the consolidated statements show an even stronger balance sheet than the statements of the individual subsidiaries</u>. The company has good banking relationships, (4) <u>especially with Jumbo Bank and The National Trust Company</u>.

Example 1: _____

Example 2: _____

Example 3: _____

Example 4: _____

Commentary: Paragraph Development

Compare your responses with these. You may have gotten some different answers in a few cases. Example 3 in Paragraph Four is both an illustration and a contrast. Example 1 in Paragraph Two is both an example and a part of the larger strategy of contrast underlying the paragraph. Not all examples of thought processes can be *absolutely* classified as one thing or another. It's only important to try to classify these processes so that *you can become more conscious of your natural ability to use them* in your thinking and, as a result, in your writing.

Paragraph One

Example 1: cause and effect analysis

Example 2: cause and effect analysis

Example 3: cause and effect analysis

Paragraph Two

Example 1: illustration

Example 2: contrast

Paragraph Three

Example 1: illustration

Example 2: cause and effect analysis

Paragraph Four

Example 1: illustration

Example 2: cause and effect analysis

Example 3: contrast

Example 4: illustration

PARAGRAPH SEQUENCING

Writers must be sure that their paragraphs follow the steps of their logic. Usually, you can trace the writer's logic through the topic sentences of paragraphs.

A topic sentence states the main idea of the paragraph. For emphasis, this sentence is usually stated at or near the beginning of the paragraph. If the topic sentence is a summary of the combined implications of a number of examples, it will be stated last or near the end of the paragraph. Rarely is a topic sentence located in the middle of the paragraph, as this would tend to deemphasize it.

Here's an example of a famous paragraph from *The Elements of Style,* one of the most successful textbooks ever written about writing.

> Vigorous writing is concise. A sentence should contain no unnecessary words, a paragraph no unnecessary sentences, for the same reason that a drawing should have no unnecessary lines and a machine no unnecessary parts. This requires not that the writer make all his sentences short, or that he avoid all detail and treat his subjects only in outline, but that every word tell.[1]

[1]William Strunk Jr., *The Elements of Style, With Revisions, an Introduction, and a Chapter on Writing by E. B. White.* Third Edition (Needham Heights, MA: Allyn & Bacon, 1979), p. 23.

You probably spotted the topic sentence. It's the first sentence. The rest of the paragraph extends and clarifies the point through explanation and specific examples.

In the following passage, the writer places topic sentences effectively both at the beginnings and ends of paragraphs. I've underlined these so that you can see the skeleton of the argument's logic.

> Recently, I met a commercial banker who told me the following: "You know, not too long ago, all that a commercial banker had to do to generate business was to handle a knife and fork and play golf." That was in the era when banks were regulated and competitors were few. <u>Today, bankers play an entirely different game.</u>
>
> <u>The banking industry has changed radically.</u> I suspect that the often-used expression "stuffy banker" will quickly die out from usage, simply because there will no longer be room for this type of individual. The traditional, relatively passive, genteel commercial bankers will, of necessity, be replaced by a tough new breed of bankers. What do I mean by "tough"?
>
> <u>I mean tough in the sense that these people will have to work much harder and smarter than their predecessors did to make money.</u> The easy days of banking are over. Today, we need men and women who not only have good social skills, but who also have superb technical skills coupled with outstanding selling ability.

A summary of these sentences yields the writer's argument: Because the banking industry is different from the way it used to be, the people who enter it must be different from the bankers of the past.

Look at another paragraph.

> Cyclical sales growth is partially controlled by continuous expansion and sufficient capitalization. Forecasting tools enable the company to plan ahead in order to control costs and protect profit margins. Quality store management and incentive programs also offset downturns to sales and/or margins. Since the company lacks diversification, cyclicality must be partially mitigated by management.

Can you find the topic sentence? Probably not. All the sentences are written in such large and general terms that any of them, or none of them, could be topic sentences. Since you cannot locate the main point of the paragraph, it's impossible to determine whether there's a sequence of logic from sentence to sentence.

The writer of this paragraph told me that his readers could "infer the meaning." But readers should not have to read your mind. In business writing, the point of a paragraph must be clearly stated and explained. Otherwise the larger logic that's being developed from paragraph to paragraph, as well as the logic within paragraphs, is not apparent to the reader, and he or she won't be able to follow the writer's "trail."

TRANSITIONS

Transitions are the signposts that help the reader follow the writer's logical trail. Without them, readers can become confused and disoriented or lose their way.

Some transitions are straightforward. Look at an example you've already seen and notice how the enumerating words *first, second,* and *third* make it easier to follow the writer's argument.

> As you are aware, a letter was released from this office regarding our new corporate policy of reporting all purchase contracts in excess of $10,000. To date, we have received no response from the manufacturing facilities. There are a number of possible explanations for this with varying implications.
>
> First, it is possible that $10,000 was an inappropriate level in that most contracts negotiated were under this level. An appropriate response to this problem would be to reassess historic purchasing levels in order to establish an appropriate threshold.
>
> Second, the problem may have resulted from the fact that the letter was released on a date too close to the peak buying season, thus not allowing the respective executives adequate time to assimilate the request into their current purchasing procedures. Should this be the case, we should begin to realize the expected benefits of the new directive when the next buying cycle begins.
>
> Third, the problem may represent a message from the purchasing executives that they resent head office tampering with their established routines. In this event, we would need to make them realize the benefits that everyone will gain if they comply with this procedure.
>
> In my opinion, the first explanation is most likely. An appropriate course of action at this point would be to arrange a conference of all the purchasing executives to discuss the problem as a group. Such a conference would also allow us to talk to each executive.

This example also illustrates another important principle: the beginning of paragraphs is usually the place to achieve a smooth transition from the previous paragraph. There will be times, however, when you'll use the end of the paragraph to provide the link to the next paragraph. For example:

> I suspect the often-used expression "stuffy banker" will quickly die out from usage, simply because there will no longer be room for this type of individual. The traditional, relatively passive, genteel commercial banker will, of necessity, be replaced by a tough new breed of bankers. What do I mean by "tough"?
>
> I mean tough in the sense that these people will have to work much harder and smarter than their predecessors to make money. The easy days of banking are over.

Picking up the thread of an idea stated at the end of one paragraph and continuing it into the next provides the needed transition.

A number of words help writers show connections between sentences and paragraphs. In using them, writers must consider carefully what kinds of relationships these words show and then what kind of relationship their particular context calls for. Here is a list of some of these words, along with the kinds of relationships they signify.

Transitional words	What Is signified
Moreover, furthermore, in addition, besides, first, second, finally	Piling up of detail
Therefore, because, according, consequently, thus, hence, as a result, so	Cause and effect relationship
Similarly, here again, likewise, in comparison, still	Comparison
Yet, conversely, whereas, nevertheless, on the other hand, however, nonetheless, but	Contrast
Although, if	Condition
For example, in particular, in this case, for instance	Illustration
Formerly, after, when, meanwhile, sometimes	Time sequence
Indeed, in fact, in any event	Intensification
That is, in other words, as has been stated	Repetition

The key to using transitions effectively is recognizing the thought processes that they signal.

Now you're going to have the opportunity to write several paragraphs in which you develop an argument. Remember: sequence the paragraphs logically and link them with transitions.

Exercise: Developing an Argument

Write three paragraphs in which you ask your boss for a raise. Assume that the raise is overdue and that you deserve it. Develop your case on the basis of *reason and logic*—for example, show the just causes why you should get the raise, present examples of your good work, compare your work in the past with your current performance to show that you've improved—whatever content makes sense for your case. *Do not* use emotional arguments such as "I need a raise because I've got a new baby on the way." We'll consider these kinds of strategies in the next lesson.

When you've finished your paragraphs, go back and underline:

- *At least one example* of illustration, comparison or contrast, and cause and effect analysis. It's almost certain that you will have used each thought process at least once.
- *One transitional bridge* between *two* of the paragraphs.
- The *topic sentence in each paragraph.*

COMMENTARY: DEVELOPING AN ARGUMENT

Although I can't give you direct commentary on your writing, I'm providing you with a sample of another person's argument along with commentary on some of the developmental techniques used, an example of a transition, and the placement of the topic sentences. I also suggest that you show your work to a friend, asking him or her to respond to it in light of the principles discussed in the lesson.

Sample Response

I've now been working with this consulting company for almost a year. During that time, I've designed and taught four major courses for two new clients, Pemper Corporation and Lifko Associates. As well as receiving uniformly excellent feedback from participants in all sessions, you yourself told me that "Jane Adamson at Pemper said Rachel Johnston came in here, psyched out this company, and delivered the kind of quality product that hasn't been seen around here in at least ten years."

As a result of these contributions I believe I should be considered for a raise. When we first began our relationship, we agreed that my per diem rate would be $200 less than my usual rate so that I could have the chance to work with you on a wider variety of projects than had been possible for me to do alone. Part of our verbal agreement also entailed my performing course needs analyses for free to help you get more business. My understanding was, however, that once we had built up enough business, you would raise my per diem rate to an appropriate fee. To date, I have helped you gain two new clients, yet I am still being paid a substandard per diem fee. I believe an appropriate raise would be $400 added to the per diem rate—$200 to bring me up to my normal rate plus a $200 merit addition.

I must also require payment in the future for the time I spend on needs analyses and will bill you at the per diem rate I charge for my other services. As you know, the last needs analysis we did for Lifko Associates required two full days of interviewing and three days to analyze the data and write the client's report. That was five days of my time I gave you for free. I realize that you don't mind doing needs analyses for clients for free—you own the company and can make up the money in terms of what you charge the client if you get the business. But I cannot be asked to work as if I'm a partner when I'm really an employee.

Examples of Paragraph Development Processes

- Cause and effect analysis: "As a result of these contributions, I believe I should be considered for a raise." (In fact, the basic argument throughout is based on cause and effect reasoning: Because I helped you build up more business, I should get a raise.)
- Contrast: "I realize that you don't mind doing needs analyses for clients for free—you own the company and can make up the money in terms of what you charge the client if you get the business. But I cannot be asked to work as if I'm a partner when I'm really an employee."
- Illustration: "Jane Adamson at Pemper said Rachel Johnston came in here, psyched out this company, and delivered the kind of quality product that hasn't been seen around here in at least ten years."

Example of Transitional Bridge

• "As a result of these contributions . . ." forms a transition from paragraph one to paragraph two.

Placement of Topic Sentences

• The topic sentences are the *first* sentence of each paragraph.

EMOTIONAL ARGUMENTS: THE ART OF PERSUASION

Emotional argumentation is not as common in business writing as in other types of writing. Generally, the subject of profit and loss is best looked at in the light of hard reason and factual observation; emotions can cloud the subject unnecessarily. Yet there are occasions when emotion plays an important and rightful part in business writing. The key is to recognize these opportunities when they present themselves and to know your audience well enough to take advantage of those opportunities.

Perhaps one of the most famous examples of recognizing the moment for emotion and knowing how to evoke it from an audience is illustrated in Marc Anthony's famous funeral oration in *Julius Caesar*.

Shakespeare dramatizes this famous occasion by having one of Caesar's murderers, Brutus, speak his eulogy first over the fallen leader. Brutus appeals to the reasonableness of the citizens, pointing out that Caesar's ambition was becoming a threat to the republic: "If then that friend demand why Brutus rose against Caesar, this is my answer—not that I loved Caesar less, but that I loved Rome more. Had you rather Caesar were living, and die all slaves, than that Caesar were dead, to live all freemen?"

Taking advantage of the opportunity to speak after Brutus, Marc Anthony calls Brutus's motives into question and whips up the crowd's emotions about the assassination:

> Here, under leave of Brutus and the rest—
> For Brutus is an honorable man,
> So are they all, all honorable men—
> Come I to speak in Caesar's funeral.
> He was my friend, faithful and just to me.
> But Brutus says he was ambitious,
> And Brutus is an honorable man.
> He hath brought many captives home to Rome,

Whose ransoms did the general coffers fill.
Did this in Caesar seem ambitious?
When that the poor have cried, Caesar hath wept—
Ambition should be made of sterner stuff.

Anthony's oration shows a knowledge of human psychology. He speaks of his own experience that Caesar was a just and honest friend. Although you might argue that logically this means little about Caesar's justness to the citizens, this same kind of argument is often used with the same success in everyday life: "X is a nice person and a good friend of mine; therefore, he would be a good candidate for this job." A personal endorsement always carries emotional weight. Similarly, the example "When that the poor have cried, Caesar hath wept" is strictly hearsay. But if you believe the speaker, as the crowd in Rome believed Anthony, you'll be likely to believe the example.

Anthony's speech illustrates that, on certain occasions, an emotional argument may be more effective than a rational one. It also illustrates that emotion is best used as an argumentative technique if it is genuine. Although Anthony probably slanted his evidence, his love for Caesar was genuine, and that feeling comes through in his speech. Emotion, when it's real and not manufactured, can be powerfully persuasive.

Let's look at a business letter that uses emotional argumentation.

Dear Governor:

I am writing to express the outcry of 70,000 hot, tired, angry New Jersey residents who try to commute every day to New York.

We are incensed over half-hearted negotiations between the Port Authority and representatives of 170 carmen.

One hundred seventy carmen!

You have declared publicly that the PATH fare must be kept at thirty cents for the welfare of New Jersey residents. The hundreds of neighbors I see every day join me in imploring you to use your office to:

1. Announce your support of a fare increase to fifty cents per ride. Even sixty cents as on the New York subway is not unreasonable.

2. Compel the Port Authority and union officials to engage in around-the-clock negotiations to reach an immediate agreement.

As long as the carmen are making nearly as much money staying at home as going to work, *why would they settle?* As long as the Port Authority is reporting a smaller deficit by not operating the PATH than by operating it, especially at a measly thirty cents, *why would they settle?* Clearly, they need some firm, pointed impetus from you. Transport of New Jersey has made an honorable attempt to provide emergency alternative service. By their own admission, though, their efforts will never match the speed and comfort of below-the-surface trans-Hudson service. Record-breaking temperatures have made the added commuting hours of the last 59 days nearly unbearable. If you truly wish to aid the welfare of New Jersey residents, intervene urgently. All 70,000 commuters and their families will be immensely grateful.

How does the writer express his emotion? First, he chooses words that express his feelings: *outcry, incensed, half-hearted, imploring, measly.* He gives concrete examples to explain his reasoning that the strike is more likely to continue than be settled: "As long as the carmen are making nearly as much money staying at home as going to work, *why would they settle?* As long as the Port Authority is reporting a smaller deficit by not operating the PATH than by operating it, especially at a measly thirty cents, *why would they settle?*" He vividly illustrates the effects of the strike on commuters: "hot, tired, angry" people for whom "record-breaking temperatures have made the added commuting hours of the last 59 days nearly unbearable."

This letter also shows the writer's knowledge of his audience's psychology. Nothing strikes more terror to the heart of a politician than unhappy, frustrated voters who blame your political inattention for their problems. By asking the governor directly for "firm, pointed impetus" in the form of "using his office" to "announce" and "compel" change, the writer implicitly challenges the reader to show that he will use his political power in a real crisis and not avoid the issue.

Perhaps the most important thing this letter illustrates is that the best use of emotion is in the service of a good cause. I mentioned some examples from *Julius Caesar* and everyday business life when emotion may be effective but not always in the service of a good cause. History shows that Julius Caesar was indeed on the road to becoming a dictator and destroying the Roman Republic. I'm sure you can think of occasions in your own life when you've seen hearsay and cronyism triumph over reason and truth. I cannot teach you to recognize a good cause. I can only trust that you will do so.

What, then, are some occasions in business that might rightfully call an emotional argument into play? Perhaps a letter or memo in which you're trying to get action on something that you perceive as unfair, hopelessly messed up, or in need of immediate attention to improve it. If you feel strongly enough about the situation, then letting your emotion show will definitely grab the readers' attention and have some kind of an effect on them. Some forms that an emotional argument might take are a letter of resignation, a "vision statement" to employees to rally them behind a new corporate strategy, or a letter addressing a commonly shared inequity in the organization to attempt to provoke political action.

Clearly, showing emotion is a risky and an often inappropriate technique in business writing. As mentioned, it can tend to cloud the factual issues of a situation—enough of this unfortunately happens in the routine performance of business without anyone adding to it. Emotion may put readers off, offend them, or, if they disagree with your position, turn them into potentially dangerous adversaries. For these reasons, most business writers avoid using emotion, especially on paper. If they are going to let their emotions show, they'll do so informally, verbally, and "off the record."

If you're going to be emotional in business writing, always keep these things in mind:

1. *Why* you think the occasion calls for an emotional appeal; and
2. *Whom* you're writing for and what is likely to be psychologically persuasive for them in this particular situation.

Finally, don't try to manufacture emotion. If it's there, you'll know it.

Exercise: Showing Emotion in Business Writing

Rewrite your report in which you asked the boss for a raise. This time, express your *feelings* about the subject. Your strategy for reaching your reader psychologically will be just as important as the language you choose. Thus before you draft the argument, write a brief sketch of the person you're writing to and include your strategy for reaching him or her psychologically. For example:

> I'm a woman writing for a person who is highly political and sensitive to events that might potentially cause him or the company trouble. As a result, one major point I need to make is that a man with exactly the same background and qualifications as mine was hired for the same job as mine at a higher salary and at a higher grade level. Mentioning sex discrimination is likely to move him to action.

For this strategy to work, *there would have to be truth* in your suggestion that you've been the possible victim of sex discrimination. Also, you'd really have to know your reader. The preceding strategy could backfire with a lot of people. It would be most likely to work with an insecure person who knows you've been wronged and who would not want you to "make a fuss," or a person who, though political, knows you've been wronged and will have a sense of fair play. While your language would be strong and perhaps threatening for the first reader, you'd use words suggesting the concepts of fairness and equality for the second reader.

COMMENTARY: SHOWING EMOTION IN BUSINESS WRITING

Once again, since I cannot provide you with direct commentary on your writing, I'm providing a sample revision. Again, the best response to your work would come from a friend or colleague, particularly someone who knows the person or kind of person you're writing for and who can therefore evaluate your strategy.

The revision here is of the argument you saw in the previous exercise. This time, the writer shows emotion. The reader is described as follows:

> I'm writing for a boss who is fair and reasonable, but who has allowed his desire for profit to cloud his judgment. Part of the reason he has neglected my raise is that he has a number of other consultants like me working for him who are willing to do needs analyses for free and take lower per diem wages than mine in order to break into the business. I need to emphasize something we both know: I'm more valuable than these people because I can do difficult assignments that they cannot do and because I have actually helped him build up business while these people have not. I may have to threaten to quit. I am *absolutely* sure that he would not want me to do that. He knows there are a number of his competitors who would love to have my services.

Sample Revision

When I first started working with your company, we agreed that my per diem rate would be $200 less than my usual rate so that I could have the chance to work with you on a wider variety of projects than had been possible for me to do alone. We also agreed, however, that if the kinds of specialized courses I design actually brought in more business, I would be raised to my usual rate plus a merit addition.

I've been working for you for almost a year now. As you know, the Pemper and Lifko accounts are a direct result of my sales and design skills. Yet I am still being paid a substandard per diem fee. I'm so upset about this that I'm on the verge of leaving. We agreed, after all, that I would be rewarded when I delivered on my promise to help you get some new clients. I've honored my end of the bargain. I think a raise that brings me up to my standard rate plus a $200 merit addition is certainly justified now.

I will also have to start charging you per diem for doing needs analysis. As things stand now, I am being asked to give large blocks of my time "for free." I realize that you and the other freelance consultants who work for you always do clients' needs analyses for free, but in the future I must require payment for the time I spend on this work. I can understand that you don't mind doing needs analyses for free—you own the company and can make up the money you lose on this service in terms of what you charge the client once they buy the course. And if other people want to give away their labor to break into consulting, that's their decision. But those people clearly have not made the contribution that I have to the company nor is there any chance that they will be able to; we both know that they don't have the skills.

I have and will continue to help you *increase* your profits. Talent, after all, is the "bottom line" in this business. But I cannot be asked to share those talents for nothing!

Comment

Even though this argument is only moderately emotional, I think you can imagine how risky it would be to write it—even for the kind of reader described. You'd have to be dead sure your services were as valuable to the boss as this person thinks they are. Otherwise, you might find yourself out of a job.

The point to remember is: always weigh *carefully* the risks of emotionalism in business writing.

CHAPTER 4

Principles of Readability

Introduction to the Principles of Readability
How Long Should a Sentence Be?
Repetition and Paragraph Logic

INTRODUCTION TO THE PRINCIPLES OF READABILITY

All writing is a recreation of someone's speaking voice. The writing's impact stems from the written voice's ability to engage, entertain, instruct, or even aggravate. The written voice, however, is not exactly the same as the spoken voice. It is a more stylized—or "controlled"—voice than the immediate speaking voice. A writer, unlike a spontaneous speaker, can consider the impact his or her voice will have in any particular situation. The writer can revise her voice, deliberate the impact of words and sentences, and even submit her written voice for appraisal before it is shared with a wider audience.

Since you've done your share of reading, you have already discovered that some written voices are easier to read than others. English prose stylists of previous centuries, for example, used long sentences, Latinate vocabulary, and elaborate allusions to the classics and the Bible. Seventeenth- and eighteenth-century readers, in particular, expected writers to "embellish" writing with these kinds of elements to enrich the context and stimulate their thinking. These readers found this kind of style "readable."

Readers today, however, have very different tastes in writing and different concepts of readability. Newspapers and magazines have greatly influenced people's concept of style. The essence of journalistic style might be described as "short and to the point." It is a highly edited, fast-paced style, suitable for helping busy readers gain a quick picture of topical stories and events.

For paper writing, journalistic style still carries great influence. The Internet and e-mail, however, have added another concept of style—the style of "paperless" writing. Unlike paper writing, which most people still conceive of as "public" writing, the Internet allows writers to express themselves informally, instantly, and with the possibility of immediate feedback.

The written voice on the Internet—especially in forums like chat groups—probably comes closest to the actual speaking voice of any written form. Whether or not this medium will radically change people's concepts of written style—even to the point of tolerating more "literacy lapses" in the service of spontaneity—no one yet knows.

At this moment, however, most readers of both paper and paperless writing expect a literate, engaging written voice to speak to them—a consciously crafted "public" voice. They also expect this voice to address them appropriately for the situation that has prompted the writing.

Another influence on modern stylistic tastes is one peculiar to people who work in organizations. This influence might be called an "internally approved style." This style is not the product of one voice, but of many voices that have communicated with each other enough to produce their own style and, to some extent, language. In fact, many large organizations develop an internal style that employees perceive as the "right way to write." Arbiters of prose style often label this kind of writing with pejorative names such as gobbledygook, officialese, bureaucratese, and The Official Style.[1] Most people would agree that this kind of writing is not easy to read. However, anyone who has ever worked in an organization can readily understand why these "official styles" of corporate life have spread and predominate in modern business writing. People choose them for self-protection and to show signs of proper conformance to the perceived standards of the organization.

The ironic situation in which many employees find themselves is that organizations seem to bless these styles with one hand and criticize and red-line them with the other. As someone often employed by organizations to teach "good writing," I encounter many people who have elected to attend my workshops primarily because they are confused by this seeming double standard. Many will tell of a boss who constantly red-lines their work for reasons they cannot understand because the changes seem highly subjective and idiosyncratic. "What," they ask, "is really the *right* way to write?"

One reason this modern Tower of Babel has resulted, I believe, is the social confusion and upheaval in which America finds itself today. Conventional answers to

[1]Richard A. Lanham, *Revising Prose* (New York: Charles Scribner's Sons, 1979), p. 25.

questions of style and usage that teachers could once utter with such authority are sometimes criticized because they do not always meet current standards of political correctness and social awareness. Is it desirable to criticize someone for ignorance of a stylistic concept that he or she had no opportunity to learn? If the message is getting across, why quibble over linguistic niceties? Why shouldn't people choose "officialese" if everyone in the organization can decipher the code? Give it to them the way they want it!

These are not easy objections to counter. Similarly, the question about the "right" way to write is not easy to answer, nor has it ever been. Why?

When you write, you must ultimately *set your own standards* and measure up to those. Education and training in writing are merely formalized ways of beginning a process that only the individual can complete. To write well, you will need to read writers whose work has stood the test of time and learn from their achievements. You will need to appraise written voices and decide what you like and do not like. You will need to educate yourself enough about the rules of writing to feel free of teachers and their dictums. You will need to consider how to address readers in view of current standards of political correctness and social awareness.

Teachers can only provide guidelines for addressing these tasks and making these important choices. The choices you make will greatly affect your ability to *communicate* your message successfully to your intended audience. Writing to communicate is not easy. To become accomplished in this way of writing means acquiring technique and not merely going on "feel," or an unthinking imitation of other people's writing and official styles, or evading conventional standards. It means being able to make your writing readable and, at the same time, palatable for different audiences and occasions.

Writing to communicate requires that you make choices about what makes writing readable. If you give up your own voice to an "official voice," or never gain enough sense of the stylistic niceties of the language to write with confidence, to some degree you have chosen to stop thinking independently. With this goes a loss of creativity and the ability to have new ideas. In fact, you may be giving up your ability to make a real contribution to your organization and to experience personal growth in your career. New ideas, problem-solving ability, and genuine innovation are the lifeblood of business.

To recognize and improve stylistic problems in your writing, you will need to experience the **impact** of writing and decide what you like and why you like it. Evaluating other people's writing is a natural way to begin developing your own style and understanding of the principles of readability. It's initially easier to be more objective about someone else's work than your own because you are the reader undergoing either a pleasurable or a painful experience.

Now you're going to have the opportunity to read and react to some examples of business writing. They are not all drawn from the same kinds of documents so their purposes are different. You will be asked only to react to the way they are written.

REACTING TO OTHER PEOPLE'S WRITING

To improve the readability of your own writing, you will first need to recognize what you like and why you like it. As a first step, read the following four paragraphs. First, circle <u>one</u> of the five descriptions that best describes your reaction to the paragraph. Then describe your reaction in a phrase of your own in the space labeled "Describe your reaction."

Example 1

While it is expected that all known and foreseeable significant credit issues will be fully dealt with and resolved in the business and strategic planning processes, it will not always be possible to adequately anticipate market opportunities and/or conditions that may occur before the next scheduled review. A business unit may want to alter its plans and establish new programs for existing or prospective markets. A change in direction that has not been included in the business and/or strategic planning process and which has significant potential for altering risk in the units' portfolio must be referred to the next higher management level for approval where the significance is weighed in terms of all the business units reporting thereto. If in that context the matter is considered significant, it is to be escalated up in accordance with the business and strategic planning processes.

(A) Clear - easy to read
(B) Clear - required some reasonable effort
(C) Clear - required substantial effort and rereading
(D) Partially Clear - required substantial rereading
(E) Unclear - tended to give up

Describe your reaction _____

Example 2

Writing is hard work. A clear sentence is no accident. Very few sentences come out right the first time, or even the third time. Remember this in moments of despair.

If you find that writing is hard, it's because it *is* hard. It's one of the hardest things people do.

  (A) Clear - easy to read
  (B) Clear - required some reasonable effort
  (C) Clear - required substantial effort and rereading
  (D) Partially Clear - required substantial rereading
  (E) Unclear - tended to give up

Describe your reaction _____

Example 3

Compensation communicates the guidelines and general philosophy of end salary positioning through the annual compensation presentation or through the Human Resources Department during salary transactions such as promotions. However, there are many factors which influence positioning end salaries, and Compensation is not always aware of these factors. On the other hand, the Human Resources Consultant knows her/his clients and is familiar with such factors. It would then make sense to have them heavily involved in the education of the end salary philosophy. The applications of this philosophy need to begin with upper management. With upper management approval, the managers will find credibility with the philosophy and begin to use it during salary transactions.

  (A) Clear - easy to read
  (B) Clear - required some reasonable effort
  (C) Clear - required substantial effort and rereading
  (D) Partially Clear - required substantial rereading
  (E) Unclear - tended to give up

Describe your reaction _____

Example 4

As part of the ongoing effort to more fully utilize the program's Spread and Projection System for production work, the Systems Committee has decided it is necessary to establish appropriate contacts with line areas and other interested parties to determine the acceptability of currently produced computerized spread reports for inclusion in production account files. It is also felt that an "internal" review of these documents would be valuable prior to the soliciting of "external" comments.

(A) Clear - easy to read
(B) Clear - required some reasonable effort
(C) Clear - required substantial effort and rereading
(D) Partially Clear - required substantial rereading
(E) Unclear - tended to give up

Describe your reaction _____

COMMENTARY

Example 1

You probably responded with D or E for the first example. Other readers have written descriptions such as

- Complex
- Not direct
- Convoluted sentences
- Vague vocabulary
- Sounds like a lawyer wrote it

To a large degree, all of these descriptions are obvious. Even though this writing is not easy to get through, this style happens a lot in business writing.

Here are some of the reasons why this kind of writing frequently happens:

- People think their writing must sound impressive.
- People think they must explain every aspect of a situation, resulting in repetitiveness.
- People write as they think rather than organizing their thoughts before they write. Or they do not revisit what they wrote to see whether editing it might improve its readability.
- People have adopted a bureaucratic style common to the company.

Example 2

Let's look at the second paragraph. This example is from a guidebook on writing entitled *On Writing Well*, Fifth Edition, by William Zinsser (New York: Harper Collins Publishers, 1994, p. 12).

You probably scored it A or B. This too is somewhat obvious. Some of the phrases other readers have used to describe it are

- clear
- direct
- conversational
- writing has punch

It's direct and easily understandable—you know what the writer is trying to tell you.

Example 3

In reacting to the third paragraph, you very well could have scored it in the D or E category. Some reactions of readers in my business writing classes are

- Main point is not clearly stated.
- Language is very abstract and jargonistic (e.g., "compensation," "end salary positioning," "salary transactions," "factors").
- Sentences are long and wordy.

However, a few Human Resources professionals have scored this paragraph A or B. They are familiar with the vocabulary and the concepts it uses. The problem is that many people are not.

Example 4

Some common reactions other readers have stated are

- I had to reread it several times to understand it.
- If I had the background for the context, I might understand this better.
- Boring
- Extremely formal
- Impersonal

There are a number of problems with this paragraph. In general, the writing is extremely slow moving. In the first sentence, the writer does not make his point until nearly the end of a 54-word sentence. More often than not, the vocabulary choices cause the reader to linger rather than grasp the writer's meaning and move on. Here are some specific examples:

- Unclear terms:
  ongoing effort—Why not just effort?
  appropriate contacts—Are some contacts inappropriate? Who?
  "internal" review—Does this mean someone within the company should read the spread reports? Who?

"external" comments—Does this mean someone outside the company, such as a consultant, will read the spread reports? Who?
- Overly fancy vocabulary choices:
  utilize, acceptability, soliciting, inclusion
- Wordy writing:
  Why "Systems Committee has decided it is necessary" rather than simply "Systems Committee decided"?
- Impersonal tone:
  "it is necessary," "it is also felt"

Note: You may have found other problems or strengths in these paragraphs. That's fine. You are becoming increasingly sensitive to what makes writing more or less readable.

HOW LONG SHOULD A SENTENCE BE?

Part of this book's purpose is to help you become more conscious of writing in a way that will be most readable to the modern business person—someone who often lacks leisure and patience.

How long should a sentence be? Just as long as a piece of string. There is no hard and fast rule that sentences must be short or long. However, as you may know, shorter sentences are generally preferred by the impatient, busy reader in business today.

Undoubtedly, the greatest influence on business writing today is journalistic style. Journalists and business people are usually writing abut the same kinds of content—facts, ideas, and opinions. Journalists and business people are also writing for the same kind of reader—the person "on the run," quickly trying to capture a coherent picture of the events of the moment. Both types of writers strive to be clear and accurate,★ as their readers will undoubtedly use the information they glean from their reading in some way.

Journalists and business writers, therefore, generally strive to write vigorously, concisely, and, most important, clearly, so that the reader will not be misled about the facts and perspective of the story or message.

Given these goals, in 1946, a man named Rudolf Flesch wrote a book that had a major impact on journalists and, later, on business writers. It was entitled *The Art of Plain Talk* and one of its major tenets was that writers should write short, uncomplicated sentences to improve the readability of their writing. Flesch was not with-

---

★I am, of course, talking about the highest standards of journalism—not "yellow journalism," which has different goals.

out his critics among journalists. Lester Markel, a former Sunday editor of *The New York Times,* cautioned against short and snappy sentences, maintaining that they "cost something in loss of clarity and perspective."[2] Nevertheless, Flesch's ideas have been extremely influential and most journalists and business writers today favor writing shorter sentences.

You will have to make your own decision about this issue. To help you, I'll first give you some "guidelines" that most good writers, whether in Flesch's camp or some more moderate camp, would endorse. Then you'll have the opportunity to improve the readability of sentences from business reports.

GUIDELINES FOR SENTENCE LENGTH

1. Be careful of long sentences (more than 18 or 20 words).

   Example: The company's new management team, after retirement of the former Chairman, has been able to turn Lyson Industries around, resulting in both a substantial working capital and equity cushion and an improved overall debt-to-equity ratio.

   Better: The new management team turned Lyson Industries around after the former Chairman retired. Now working capital and equity are substantial. The debt-to-equity ratio has also improved.

As this example illustrates, you can:

- Break the sentence apart with commas and periods to achieve <u>sentences of various lengths</u>. They add rhythm and emphasis to your prose.
- Rearrange the sentence and change words to achieve clarity.

2. Be careful of sentences composed of the verb *to be* (is, are, was, were) and a long string of prepositional phrases.

   Example: An example *of* financial advisory services *at* Jumbo Bank *is* the provision *of* these services *to* low-income households.

   Better: For example, Jumbo Bank provides financial advisory services to low-income households.

When faced with this problem, you can:

- Get rid of the verb *is* and substitute a verb with life in it. You'll usually find that some other word in the sentence contains the root that should be the sentence's main verb (in this case, the word *provision*).

[2]Obituary of Dr. Rudolf Flesch, *The New York Times,* October 7, 1986, B7.

- Rearrange the sentence and eliminate as many prepositions as possible. When you eliminate a preposition, you either eliminate its object or find a new place for the object. Remember, prepositions always have objects: to the *store,* at the *door,* of the *group,* on *time,* etc.

3. Be careful of sentences hooked to other sentences with semicolons, colons, and dashes. These specialized punctuation marks should be used sparingly. The period and the comma should be your major punctuation marks.

Example: Changing financial markets have caused most banks to change their marketing strategies; examples of some of these strategies include: creating a consulting department; targeting medium-sized companies as customers because they are more likely to need consulting services; increasing credit card services because of their high interest rates; and increasing investment banking transactions which are more profitable.

Better: Banks are selling new products and services because financial markets have changed. One new service is financial consulting to medium-sized companies. Since credit cards carry high interest rates, banks are increasing this line of business. Many are also making highly profitable investment banking deals.

As this example shows, you can:

- Break the sentence into sentences of various lengths.
- Add, change, rearrange, or delete words to achieve clarity.
- Punctuate with the comma and the period.

Exercise: Writing Readable Sentences

Here are four unnecessarily long sentences. The thought in each is clear, it just takes the reader too much effort to understand it.

Rewrite each sentence so that the thought may be more easily understood.

Your major tools are

- use of punctuation, primarily the period and comma, to achieve sentences of various lengths;
- eliminating the verb *to be* (is, are, was, were) in sentences where it is accompanied by a string of prepositional phrases; and
- adding, changing, rearranging, or deleting words to achieve clarity.

1. Although some of us who are familiar with the requested deal have definite reservations about the procedure required, we have to admit that something different has

been introduced into the relationship between the customer and his financier which will have a result that as yet we have been unable to predict.

2. Any assistance you require from our Construction Department will be made available upon request if you will just call us at 583-1274; if you have any questions regarding the attached draft as well, please call the same number.

3. The important preparation for Lyco Bank to take prior to the deregulation is in positioning for immediate entry into the new fields of business.

4. We not only have duplications of some tasks under the present system, but each clerk has developed his own work routines and this causes confusion which could be avoided by having a uniform method of processing paperwork.

SAMPLE REVISION: WRITING READABLE SENTENCES

Compare your revisions with these. Keep in mind that these are only suggestions. Which do you like better? To what degree does each illustrate the principles we talked about? A number of responses may be possible, and you may come up with a better one than these.

1. Some of us who are familiar with the requested deal have definite reservations about the procedure required. We have to admit, however, that something different

has been introduced into the relationship between the customer and his financier. What the ultimate result will be we have not yet been able to predict.

2. If you have any questions about the attached draft or need help from the Construction Department, call 583-1274.

3. Lyco Bank should prepare to enter new fields of business before deregulation occurs.

4. Some tasks are duplicated under the present system and each clerk has developed his own work routines. A uniform method of processing paperwork would eliminate confusion.

Causes and Cures for Wordiness

When you responded earlier to some other people's writing (see pages 70 to 72), you probably noticed that several of the paragraphs contained a number of long sentences. You may have indicated that these sentences hindered your reading and comprehension of the paragraph.

Let's take a look at some of the causes of long sentences. We'll consider the most obvious causes first. They are

- Unnecessary words
- Repeating or belaboring a point

These problems are sometimes referred to as *wordiness.*

There are two cures for these problems. One is being organized and clear about what you have to say before you write. The other is editing after you write.

It would seem that the first cure is the obvious and appropriate one. Yet even the best writers are not crystal clear about their thoughts when they first sit down to write. Writing is an act of exploration and discovery. We often find out what we think as we write.

Thus, for most of us, the first attempt is not the final product. It must be refined, re-arranged, clarified—in short, *edited.*

To bring about the second cure, you must become an editor of your own work. This means becoming objective about the presence of wordiness in your writing and not being overly attached to every word you write. It also means taking the time to revise the first draft.

In short, don't worry about being wordy as you write. You may experience "writer's block" if you write and edit simultaneously. But do take the time to edit your work after you've written. Learning to edit means recognizing the presence of certain problems and knowing ways to improve or change what's causing them.

Perhaps the most common cause of wordiness is unnecessary words. By *unnecessary* I mean words that are not essential to convey the sentence's meaning clearly.

Unnecessary words come in different guises. The most common offenders are articles (*the, a,* and *an*) and prepositions (*to, for, from, in order to, in addition to, of,* etc.). Other kinds, such as the word *that,* can be determined in context.

Here's an example of a short, simple sentence that contains unnecessary words:

essential essential   (optional)   essential

Steve is ~~an~~ (especially) intelligent ~~person~~.
          unnecessary   unnecessary

This analysis shows that the article *an* and the noun *person* are not necessary for the sentence's thought to be clearly conveyed. *Especially* is a qualifying word that may be necessary to preserve a certain shade of meaning the writer intended.

Thus you might say a sentence contains three classes of words:

Essential words: Those that *must* be written to convey the thought.

Optional words: Those that *may* be used to qualify essential words.

Unnecessary words: Those that are not needed because *they say nothing.*

Another type of wordiness comes from the notion that "two words will make the point better than one."

1. Continuing with this project is *useless* and *futile.* (double adjective)
2. The company may *modify* and *change* its business plan. (double verb)

Repetition of this kind does not emphasize the point but merely serves to slow the reader down.

Exercise: Eliminating Unnecessary Words

In these three sentences, find all of the unnecessary words you can and <u>cross them out</u>. Do not attempt to rearrange the sentences, though some rearrangement also might improve them. Concentrate on simply finding the unnecessary words.

1. Smith thinks that the company policy which was designed to cover this matter is obsolete and no longer used.

2. We must not permit ourselves to lose out on these new customers, even if it turns out that we must replace all of their old coffee pots in order to satisfy them.

3. There has been a mishandling of the funds which represents what might be con-

sidered collusion on the part of the bookkeeper and his assistant, although both of them advise that, while the procedure they engaged in is certainly a relatively uncommon one, neither of them sees how his own actions in it can be considered in any way reprehensible or otherwise deserving of censure.

SUGGESTED REVISIONS: ELIMINATING UNNECESSARY WORDS

Notice that I've merely deleted the unnecessary words. No attempt to change the basic sentence structure has been made yet.

1. Smith thinks ~~that~~ the company policy ~~which was~~ designed to cover this ~~matter~~ is obsolete ~~and no longer used~~.

2. We must not ~~permit ourselves to~~ lose ~~out on~~ these new customers, even if ~~it turns out that~~ we must replace all ~~of~~ their old coffee pots ~~in order~~ to satisfy them.

3. There has been a mishandling of ~~the~~ funds which ~~represents what~~ might be considered collusion ~~on the part~~ of the bookkeeper and his assistant, although both ~~of them~~ advise that, while the procedure ~~they engaged in~~ is ~~certainly~~ a *(optional)* (relatively) uncommon ~~one~~, neither ~~of them~~ sees how his ~~own~~ actions ~~in it~~ can be considered ~~in any way~~ reprehensible ~~or otherwise deserving of censure~~.

REPETITION AND PARAGRAPH LOGIC

Repetition of words or phrases is not difficult to recognize. Sometimes you must repeat an idea, word, or phrase to be clear. It requires judgment to decide whether repetition helps or detracts from clarity.

Sometimes it's surprising to see how much repetition occurs in a seemingly short and simple piece of writing. A high degree of repetition usually indicates a need for editing.

> The *Board of Directors* of the *Company* authorized a *3-for-1 stock split* for *shareholders* of record on June 1, 1997. This *3-for-1 split* is the first *stock split* the *Company* has had in 32 years. A *3-for-1 split* means that 2 additional *shares* will be issued for each *share* held. The *Board of Directors* will publish a *shareholder's* letter next week announcing this *stock split*.

The number of repeated words is amazing, isn't it? This usually results from writing without an organized idea of what you want to say. Thus the logic is unclear.

As a first step toward eliminating these kinds of repetitions, you have to determine what is wrong with the original organization. By rethinking the writing's logic, you will usually discover a way to combine ideas and thereby eliminate redundancies.

Exercise: Revised Order of Importance

Arrange the ideas in this paragraph from *most important to least important* order. Keep in mind that the paragraph is intended to be the opening of a public relations release previewing the stock split.

Here's the main idea of each sentence, summarized:

Sentence 1. A split has been authorized.

Sentence 2. It's the first split in 32 years.

Sentence 3. Definition of what a 3-for-1 split means.

Sentence 4. A letter next week will announce the authorization of the stock split.

Reorder the ideas in most important least important order:

Most important idea _____

_____

Next important idea _____

_____

Next important idea _____

_____

Least important idea _____

_____

COMMENTARY: REVISED ORDER OF IMPORTANCE

Sentence 1. A split has been authorized.

Sentence 2. A letter next week will announce the authorization of the stock split.

Sentence 3. It's the first split in 32 years.

Sentence 4. Definition of what a 3-for-1 split means.

A major problem with the first version is that it seems as though the writer suddenly remembered the existence of the forthcoming announcement letter too late in the writing process and stuck in the last sentence as a kind of afterthought. In terms of priority, however, the publication of the letter "next week" containing the announcement is more important in a public relations release than an historical fact such as "it is the first split in 32 years." This and the definition of a 3-for-1 split are minor points compared with the announcement of the split and the time and means by which the announcement will be made.

When an important point is out of order or stuck in as an afterthought, the writer is clearly disorganized and merely writing as things pop into mind. The result is invariably *repetitiveness*.

Now, using your new order, rewrite the paragraph and eliminate as many repetitions as you can.

Exercise: Eliminating Repetition

The *Board of Directors* of the *Company* authorized a *3-for-1 stock split* for *shareholders* of record on June 1, 1997. This *3-for-1 split* is the first *stock split* the *Company* has had in 32 years. A *3-for-1 split* means that 2 additional *shares* will be issued for each *share* held. The *Board of Directors* will publish a *shareholder's* letter next week announcing this *stock split*.

Revised Order of Importance

Sentence 1. A split has been authorized.

Sentence 2. A letter next week will announce the authorization of the stock split.

Sentence 3. It's the first split in 32 years.

Sentence 4. Definition of what a 3-for-1 split means.

Your Revision:

_____

_____

_____

_____

_____

SUGGESTED REVISION: ELIMINATING REPETITION

Consider this revision of the paragraph. Once again, this is not the only possible answer. Use this as a guide in assessing your response.

> The Board of Directors will publish a letter next week announcing a 3-for-1 stock split for shareholders of record, June 1, 1997. This split, the first in 32 years, means 2 shares will be issued for each one held.

ELIMINATING REPETITION AND BELABORING

Repetition and belaboring a point go hand in hand. It's often difficult to separate them clearly in a context, for they stem from the same cause—disorganization.

Three steps used by editors can help you identify and eliminate these problems:

1. Identify all repetitious words and phrases.
2. Identify all sentences that repeat all or part of the same idea.
3. Identify words that are unnecessary.

Exercise: Eliminating Repetition and Belaboring

To help you practice these important skills, read the following paragraph and do three things:

1. Circle all words and short phrases (except pronouns) that are repeated *more than once*. Pronouns will naturally be repeated more often.
2. Circle any parts of sentences or whole sentences that seem to *belabor the same point* unnecessarily.
3. Cross out unnecessary words.

1 On June 2, we paid a visit to the Rose Garden Apartment Complex.

2 We met John Smith, the superintendent of the complex. It seems

3 that they have about the same problems as we do, but not on as

4 large a scale, due to the fact that they are a smaller complex.

5 One of their ideas, which is very good, is their security of

6 tenants' keys. They are tagged according to the tenant's

7 social security number. This system, we felt, is good because

8 if a key is lost it cannot be traced to the tenant's residence.

9 The system we have now has the tenant's address tagged on the

10 keys. If one of our keys is lost with the tenant's address on

11 it, someone could find the key and we could find ourselves in a

12 very embarrassing position.

SUGGESTED REVISIONS: ELIMINATING REPETITION AND BELABORING

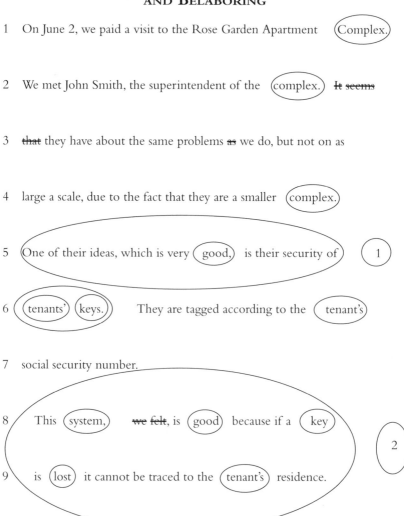

1   On June 2, we paid a visit to the Rose Garden Apartment ~~Complex.~~

2   We met John Smith, the superintendent of the ~~complex.~~ ~~It seems~~

3   ~~that~~ they have about the same problems ~~as~~ we do, but not on as

4   large a scale, due to the fact that they are a smaller ~~complex.~~

5   ~~One of their ideas, which is very ~~good,~~ is their security of~~ 1

6   ~~tenants'~~ ~~keys.~~ They are tagged according to the ~~tenant's~~

7   social security number.

8   This ~~system,~~ ~~we felt,~~ is ~~good~~ because if a ~~key~~

9   is ~~lost~~ it cannot be traced to the ~~tenant's~~ residence.

2

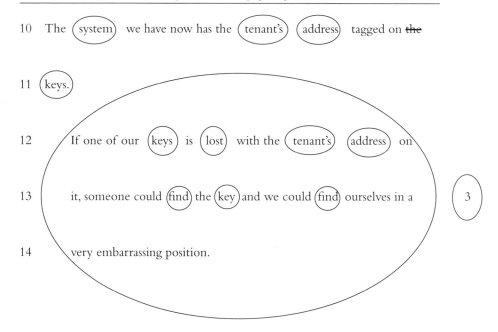

10   The (system) we have now has the (tenant's) (address) tagged on ~~the~~

11   (keys.)

12   If one of our (keys) is (lost) with the (tenant's) (address) on

13   it, someone could (find) the (key) and we could (find) ourselves in a   3

14   very embarrassing position.

COMMENTARY

Compare your analysis to this one. You probably caught most of the repeated words.

Surprisingly, there are not too many words you can cross out without creating "non-sentences." However, if you had been allowed to rearrange and combine sentences, you could probably have eliminated lots of excess words.

The belabored point occurs in three sentences: lines 5-6, 8-9, and 12-14. These three sentences are basically saying all or part of the same idea:

- Tagging tenants' keys with their social security numbers rather than their address is a good idea because if the key is lost it cannot be traced back to the owner's residence.

Exercise: Combining Editorial Techniques

Once you've done these three editorial steps, you are now ready to "clean up." Assume that the logic is okay. This time, rearrange and combine sentences as much as you like. You should be able to eliminate a lot of repetition and wordiness.

1 On June 2, we paid a visit to the Rose Garden Apartment Complex.

2 We met John Smith, the superintendent of the complex. It seems

3 that they have about the same problems as we do, but not on as

4 large a scale, due to the fact that they are a smaller complex.

5 One of their ideas, which is very good, is their security of

6 tenants' keys. They are tagged according to the tenant's

7 social security number. This system, we felt, is good because

8 if a key is lost it cannot be traced to the tenant's residence.

9 The system we have now has the tenant's address tagged on the

10 keys. If one of our keys is lost with the tenant's address on

11 it, someone could find the key and we could find ourselves in a

12 very embarrassing position.

Your Revision

_____

_____

_____

_____

_____

SUGGESTED REVISION: COMBINING EDITORIAL TECHNIQUES

Compare your revision to this one. Obviously, it is only one of many possible versions. The point is to eliminate the large number of repetitions and keep the basic message intact. If your version does this, it's fine.

visited   on June 2 and

1 ~~On June 2,~~ We ~~paid a visit to~~ the Rose Garden Apartment Complex^

complex's
2 ~~We~~ met John Smith, the ^ superintendent ~~of the complex. It seems~~

a smaller
3 ~~that~~ They have about the same problems ~~as~~ we do, but ~~not~~ on ~~as~~ ^

because
4 ~~large a~~ scale, ~~due to the fact that~~ they are a smaller complex.

idea
5 One ~~of their ideas, which is~~ very good ^ is their security of

which   **by**
6 tenants' keys ~~They~~ are tagged ~~according to the tenant's~~

7 social security number. ~~This system, we felt, is good because~~

8 ~~if a key is lost it cannot be traced to the tenant's residence.~~

9 ~~The system~~ We have ~~now has~~ the tenant's address tagged on ~~the~~

10 keys. If one ~~of our keys~~ is lost ~~with the tenant's address on~~

it   **be**
11 ~~it~~, someone could find ~~the key~~ and we could ~~find ourselves in a~~

embarrassed
12 ~~very embarrassing position~~.

Here's the above revision reprinted:

> We visited the Rose Garden Apartment Complex on June 2 and met John Smith, the Complex's superintendent. They have about the same problems we do, but on a smaller scale, because they are a smaller complex. One very good idea is their security of tenants' keys which are tagged by social security number. We have the tenant's address tagged on keys. If one is lost, someone could find it and we could be embarrassed.

CHAPTER 5

Clarifying Your Voice

Recognizing Active and Passive Voice
The Habit of Passive Writing
To Use or Not to Use Passive Voice

RECOGNIZING ACTIVE AND PASSIVE VOICE

Read these two paragraphs on the same subject. Be aware of the degree of wordiness in each and the impact of the wordiness on you as a reader.

EXAMPLE 1

Dear Congressman:

Your assistance in utilizing both congressional and appropriate Government office pressure to bring an end to the PATH strike, now in its 53rd day, would be sincerely welcomed by both your constituents and those constituents of other members of the New Jersey Congressional Delegation. The very fact that 80,000 New Jersey commuters have been seriously inconvenienced for this long space of time indicates the vital necessity of Government intervention. The New York subway strike was settled in a minimum amount of time, whereas the PATH strike has not received the attention of any Governmental organization. For your information the additional expense of commuting via bus and New York City subway has increased my commuting expense to $105.00 monthly, an intolerable burden.

EXAMPLE 2

Dear Congressman:

Your constituents need you to bring pressure to end the PATH strike. The New York City Government settled its strike quickly, but no Governmental organization in New Jersey has paid any attention to the PATH strike. I, like 80,000 other New Jersey commuters, am very upset. I now pay $105.00 a month in commuting expenses, an intolerable burden.

By now, you have become much more sensitive to writing that is readable and probably recognized that the second paragraph speaks more directly to you. It more readily captures your attention than the first. In this case the writer wanted action on the PATH strike, therefore getting the congressman's attention was probably a good idea.

A major difference between these two paragraphs is that the first is written in passive voice and the second is written in active voice.

In **active voice,** a sentence's subject does something.

Active: John Smith called the employees.

The subject of this sentence is "John Smith." Note that "John Smith" is the person *doing* the calling.

In passive voice, a sentence's subject does not *do* an action; it is *acted upon*.

Passive: The employees were called by John Smith.

In this example, the subject of the sentence is "employees." Note that the employees are *not doing* the calling. Thus this sentence is passive.

Consider the following:

Example 1

A survey was conducted in 1996 in cooperation with the American Society of Financial Planners to gather information about financial service employees.

It's written in passive voice. Now ask yourself, Who did the survey?

You probably hesitated before answering. This sentence does not identify who initiated the survey. As often happens with passive voice, that information was omitted.

In active voice, this writer must identify who did what.

Example 2

> In 1996, I <u>conducted</u> a survey with the American Society of Financial Planners to gather information about financial service employees.

It is much easier to understand what happened in this example because the doer of the action is placed before the verb. In passive sentences, the doer is placed behind the verb—or omitted entirely. In fact, passive voice may be popular with some writers because it offers them the opportunity to bury or lose the "doer."

> Reports <u>were presented</u> by the Construction Department that the superstructure was defective.

> Reports <u>were presented</u> that the superstructure was defective.

> It <u>was reported</u> by the Construction Department that the superstructure was defective.

> It <u>was reported</u> that the superstructure was defective.

> <u>There was a report</u> by the Construction Department stating that the superstructure was defective.

> <u>There was a report</u> stating that the superstructure was defective.

Although occasions will arise when you won't want to identify the doer of an action, most of the time you will. Clarity in writing comes from identifying the players in a situation. You should only lose or bury the doer of an action when

- *What* is done is more important than *who* did it; or
- You purposely want to emphasize the action or de-emphasize the doer.

Consider these two sentences:

> Active: Eve gave Adam the apple.

> Passive: The apple was given by Eve to Adam.

The passive sentence focuses your attention on *the apple* rather than on Eve. Eve could even be omitted:

> Passive: The apple was given to Adam.

Now Eve is off the hook—at least for the moment. If you wanted to hide her role in this event, you'd choose the passive. If you wanted to highlight her part, you'd choose the active.

Ultimately, it's where you want readers to focus their attention that determines whether you voice an idea actively or passively. These choices are made subliminally. Problems result when writers choose the passive more from habit than from considerations of tone and emphasis.

Active voice can add other value to your writing. It often yields a more concise, direct statement than passive voice. Passive voice can be wordy when it requires adding a prepositional phrase to identify the action's doer.

Passive: The world <u>is seen</u> *by the human eye* in a variety of colors.

Active: The human eye <u>sees</u> the world in a variety of colors.

In the final analysis, however, active and passive voice are stylistic choices. It's important for writers to use active voice *when they wish to* and passive voice *when they wish to.*

Before this can happen, you must recognize easily when a verb is in active voice and when it's in passive voice. Then you can choose between these options to voice your message most appropriately for your audience.

Exercise: Recognizing Active and Passive Sentences

Indicate whether the next ten sentences are active or passive by putting A or P in the line provided. Refer back to the definition examples if you need to.

1. The accountant made an error in his calculations. _____

2. The check was given to John three days late. _____

3. Your contribution will be appreciated. _____

4. Economies of scale were closely observed by the company. _____

5. The company's economies of scale contributed to its bottom-line

    profit. _____

6. Your interest in my resume is greatly appreciated. _____

7. I recommend that we offer this company a line of credit. _____

8. The vice president took charge of the company's overseas

    operation. _____

9. It was noted that the committee gave its recommendations on the

    project. ——————————

10. The boxer was knocked out by his opponent. _____

Answer: Recognizing Active and Passive Sentences

1. The accountant made an error in his calculations. _____A_____

2. The check was given to John three days late. _____P_____

3. Your contribution will be appreciated. _____P_____

4. Economies of scale were closely observed by the company. _____P_____

5. The company's economies of scale contributed to its bottom-line profit.

    _____A_____

6. Your interest in my resume is greatly appreciated. _____P_____

7. I recommend that we offer this company a line of credit. _____A_____

8. The vice president took charge of the company's overseas operation.

    _____A_____

9. It was noted that the committee gave its recommendations on the project.

    _____P_____

10. The boxer was knocked out by his opponent. _____P_____

THE HABIT OF PASSIVE WRITING

It's easy to recognize active and passive voice when isolated examples are shown. Now try the following paragraph.

Exercise: Recognizing Passive Verbs

Underline all of the verbs you think are passive.

1) The International Monetary System that prevailed

2) in the postwar period until 1971 was conceived at

3) the Bretton Woods Conference of 1944. Monetary

4) experts had two major objectives. First, it was

5) hoped that they could create a system which would

6) eliminate the worst features of the system that

7) prevailed during the interwar period, especially

8) devices such as competitive exchange devaluations

9) and exchange controls. (These two devices had been

10) resorted to by most of the major economies of the

11) world in an attempt to increase employment and reverse

12) the economic decline of the depression.) Second,

13) it was desired that the system would allow countries

14) to have a degree of independence in pursuing domestic

15) economic policy. It can be recalled from the previous

16) section of this module that fixed exchange rates, if

17) rigidly enforced, can lead to domestic unemployment

18) and other unwanted internal effects.

COMMENTARY: RECOGNIZING PASSIVE VERBS

The passage contains five passive verbs:

1) The International Monetary System that prevailed

2) in the postwar period until 1971 <u>was conceived</u> at
   (1)

3) the Bretton Woods Conference of 1944. Monetary

4) experts had two major objectives. First, <u>it was</u>

5) <u>hoped</u> that they could create a system which would
   (2)

6) eliminate the worst features of the system that

7) prevailed during the interwar period, especially

8) devices such as competitive exchange devaluations

9) and exchange controls. (These two devices had been
   (3)
10) resorted to by most of the major economies of the

11) world in an attempt to increase employment and reverse

12) the economic decline of the depression.) Second,
    (4)
13) it was desired that the system would allow countries

14) to have a degree of independence in pursuing domestic
    (5)
15) economic policy. It can be recalled from the previous

16) section of this module that fixed exchange rates, if

17) rigidly enforced, can lead to domestic unemployment

18) and other unwanted internal effects.

This passage illustrates what frequently happens when the writer begins to write in passive voice. Whole paragraphs and, indeed, whole sections of a document are written totally with passive sentences and verbs of being (*is, was, were*), which also express no action.

I can only guess at the reasons for this "habit of passive writing." What probably happens is that once writers put their feet on the path of passive sentence structure, they unconsciously become fully committed to the inverted patterns and longer length of passive sentences. In fact, their ears may come to find these longer rhythms more "elegant" than the shorter, staccato rhythms of active sentences.

Another contributing element to consistently passive writing may be a dim memory most people have of being told by their English teacher to keep their tenses (past, present, future, etc.) consistent in a paragraph. There's no rule, however, that says voice must be consistent with tense in a paragraph. Do not confuse the two.

I think you can see from these examples that large-scale use of passive voice lengthens sentences, increases wordiness, and makes understanding the message more difficult.

TECHNIQUES FOR REVISING PASSIVE VOICE

Changing passive voice to active voice can be challenging, especially if a passage or entire document is primarily passive. When you decide a sentence or passage relies too heavily on passive voice, you have several options for revision.

Turn the Passive Clause or Sentence Around

Here are two steps to revise passive clauses and sentences:

1. Find the prepositional phrase after the verb that identifies the doer of the action.
2. Make the object of the prepositional phrase the subject of the active clause or sentence.

Example: The roll-out conferences are arranged <u>by the Educational Coordinator</u> through the Academy's Educational Committee.

The Educational Coordinator <u>arranges</u> the roll-out conferences through the Academy's Educational Committee.

Sometimes, there is no prepositional phrase. The doer is simply omitted from the sentence. In such cases, you must insert the doer.

Example: Two parallel tests to ensure that the coding properly responds to all user-initiated events <u>were conducted.</u>

The <u>quality-assurance team conducted</u> two parallel tests to ensure that the coding properly responds to all user-initiated events.

Find a Different Verb

Sometimes, another word in the sentence contains the root of a better verb.

Example: The chemical process was always observed to *decompose* the substance into five elements.

The chemical process *decomposes* the substance into five elements.

Rethink the Sentence

You can often simplify a sentence by rethinking what you want to say. You can usually eliminate the passive construction, especially in long, complicated sentences.

Example: Marketing programs targeted to landscape architects could be better *focused* if the sources of plant material information *used* by landscape architects to make decisions *are understood* by nurserymen.

Nurserymen *can better market* landscape architects if they *know* what types of informational resources landscape architects *use.*

Make the Subject a Concrete Noun

If you find yourself using too many personal pronouns, substitute concrete nouns as the subject of the sentence.

Examples: This *report* tabulates the results of a study . . .

The *technician* first removes . . .

Tests show that . . .

The *task force* discovered that . . .

The following *chart* classifies . . .

These examples all use subjects that are either people on the project (technician, task force) or something that demonstrates the findings (reports, tests, charts).

Exercise: Eliminating the Passive Voice

Now you'll have the opportunity to rewrite the passive passage we discussed in active voice. Be especially conscious of improving the *clarity* and *readability* of the writing. For example, if a prepositional phrase has been dropped and you can *infer from context* what its object would have been, decide whether or not making that object the subject of the new active sentence would improve clarity and readability.

1) The International Monetary System that prevailed
                  (1)
2) in the postwar period until 1971 <u>was conceived</u> at
3) the Bretton Woods Conference of 1944. Monetary
4) experts had two major objectives. First, <u>it was</u>
   (2)
5) <u>hoped</u> that they could create a system which would
6) eliminate the worst features of the system that
7) prevailed during the interwar period, especially
8) devices such as competitive exchange devaluations
9) and exchange controls. (These two devices <u>had been</u>
    (3)
10) <u>resorted to</u> by most of the major economies of the
11) world in an attempt to increase employment and reverse
12) the economic decline of the depression.) Second,
    (4)
13) <u>it was desired</u> that the system would allow countries
14) to have a degree of independence in pursuing domestic
       (5)
15) economic policy. <u>It can be recalled</u> from the previous
16) section of this module that fixed exchange rates, if

17) rigidly enforced, can lead to domestic unemployment

18) and other unwanted internal effects.

Your Revision:

_____

_____

_____

_____

_____

SUGGESTED REVISION: ELIMINATING THE PASSIVE VOICE

1) Monetary experts conceived[(1)] the International Monetary

2) System at the Bretton Woods Conference in 1944. They

3) had two major objectives. First, they hoped[(2)] they could

4) create a system which would eliminate the worst

5) features of the system that prevailed during the

6) interwar period, especially devices such as

7) competitive exchange devaluations and exchange

8) controls. (Most of the major economies of the world

9) had resorted[(3)] to these two devices in an attempt to in-

10) crease employment and reverse the decline of the

11) depression.) Second, they desired[(4)] that the system

12) would allow countries to have a degree of independence

13) in pursuing domestic economic policy. You may recall[(5)]

14) from the previous section of this module that fixed

15) exchange rates, if rigidly enforced, can lead to

16) domestic unemployment and other unwanted internal

17) effects.

COMMENTARY: ELIMINATING THE PASSIVE VOICE

Notice that the editor inferred from context what the subjects of the active sentences should be for examples 1, 4, and 5. In example 5, the editor had to figure out that the paragraph is from a reading such as a textbook or training manual (the word "module" is a clue). The subject of the last sentence could also be written "The reader may recall." This would not, however, be as direct as the construction "You may recall."

In all five cases, using active voice improves the clarity and directness of the sentences. If active voice had been used together with some of the other editing techniques you've studied, the sentences could have been improved even more.

As we've already discussed, however, there is no law that says you must use active voice as opposed to passive voice. The choice is made on the basis of your purpose in the sentence or paragraph.

Exercise: Achieving Clarity through Active Voice

Underline the passive verbs in the following passage. Then revise the passage to improve its clarity. You may also use editing techniques to eliminate wordiness, repetition, or long sentences.

Example 1

The following procedure is recommended for your use.

Your PC should be shut down at the end of the day. To ensure that a proper shut down has been achieved, the switches on the terminal, printer, and powerline strip should be checked and turned off. It should be turned on again only by the person assigned the log-on code for its use.

Example 2

Since James Quiet is currently performing this task, training will need to be scheduled with James to learn the steps involved and the kinds of data that is required from the client. I would like to recommend that a training plan be developed by James documenting the procedures and time frames involved in both a new solicitation and a takeover of business. We can make arrangements to have this training include both myself and a backup, or, have it be conducted only with myself and I would then be responsible for training a backup.

Example 3

During the course of our audit, it was noted that certain accrued expense accounts were not being analyzed on a timely basis. To help ensure the propriety of all accrued expense account balances, analyses of all such accounts should be prepared periodically by you. These analyses should be reviewed and approved by the appropriate management personnel.

COMMENTARY: ACHIEVING CLARITY THROUGH ACTIVE VOICE

Compare your revisions with the sample revisions. A number of responses are possible, and yours may be just as good or better than these.

Example 1

The following procedure <u>is recommended</u> for your use.

Your PC <u>should be shut down</u> at the end of the day. To ensure that a proper shut down <u>has been achieved</u>, the switches on the terminal, printer, and powerline strip <u>should be checked and turned off</u>. <u>It should be turned on again</u> only by the person assigned the log-on code for its use.

Sample Revision

At the end of the day, you should:

• *Turn off the switches* on the terminal, printer, and powerline strip.

Only the person assigned the log-on code should turn on the PC again.

Example 2

Since James Quiet is currently performing this task, training <u>will need to be scheduled</u> with James to learn the steps involved and the kinds of data that <u>is required</u> from the client. I would like to recommend that a training plan <u>be developed</u> by James documenting the procedures and time frames involved in both a new solicitation and a takeover of business. We can make arrangements to have this training include both myself and a backup, or, have it <u>be conducted</u> only with myself and I would then be responsible for training a backup.

Sample Revision

Since James Quiet performs this task, I recommend he develop a training plan to teach the steps of the task and the kinds of data we must get from the client. The plan should include the procedures and time frames involved in both a new solicitation and a takeover of business. Then we have two options:

- train me and a backup, or
- train me and let me train my own backup.

Example 3

During the course of our audit, <u>it was noted</u> that certain underwriters' expense accounts <u>were not being analyzed</u> on a timely basis. To help ensure the propriety of all expense account balances, analyses of all such accounts <u>should be prepared</u> periodically by you. These analyses <u>should be reviewed and approved</u> by the appropriate management personnel.

Sample Revision

Our audit shows that not all underwriters' expense accounts <u>are being analyzed</u>. [passive verb] To ensure the propriety of all expense account balances, you must analyze all these accounts periodically. Managers must then review and approve these analyses.

Note: In this revision, the writer chose to leave one passive verb. In the first sentence, the important point is that the accrued expense accounts are not all being analyzed. *What is being done is more important than who is doing it.* It's not necessary to point the finger at someone until the second sentence.

TO USE OR NOT TO USE PASSIVE VOICE

Most business writers prefer the normal word order of active voice. Sometimes, however, they will prefer to use passive voice. Why?

Passive voice is a better choice in business writing when:

1. You *truly* need to be tactful and must omit who did something—you're not merely covering yourself.
2. You want to focus on an idea rather than on the person who had the idea (usually yourself).
3. You must write "politically." For example, you are writing to a "hostile" reader who is more powerful than you in the company.

Some examples will clarify these points.

TACTFULNESS

Passive: Journal entry errors were made in the books.

Active: Our accountant made journal entry errors in the books.

If there's no need to make trouble for the accountant, then you would probably choose the passive sentence.

FOCUS ON "WHAT WAS DONE"

Passive: A secured loan will be offered to the customer.

Active: I will offer the customer a secured loan.

If it's important to identify who will offer the loan (you, in this case), you'll choose active voice. If it isn't—for example, the sentence is part of an internal memo at the bank and it's clear who is making the offer—you'll probably use passive voice.

POLITICAL WRITING

Passive: Several objections have been raised as a result of some points made at the last task force meeting.

Active: The task-force members raised several objections to your points made at the last meeting.

If your objective is basically to slow down the reader's comprehension of negative or sensitive issues, then you'll use passive voice. In this example, the first sentence (in passive voice) omits the source of the objection, whereas the active sentence highlights the source. If the reader has power over the task-force members and could make trouble for them, it makes sense to raise objections to his or her ideas carefully and slowly.

A word of warning about political writing. Some business writers write as if every report, letter, and proposal is a volatile political situation. Thus their style is always passive, circumlocutive, and turgid. I believe such a habit is unnecessary; surely every writing situation we face on our jobs is not fraught with political danger.

Exercise: Passive or Active?

In each of these pairs of sentences, one is active and one is passive.

First, put an A next to the active sentence and P next to the passive sentence.

Then, identify in the space provided which voice you would use for the particular reader or readers described and briefly explain why.

1. Profits were increased by Burco Inc. in 1996. _____

2. Burco Inc. increased its profits in 1996. _____

Which voice would you use for:

A report to a current investor thinking of buying Burco stock?

_____ Voice

Why? _____

_____

A report to current stockholders?

_____ Voice

Why? _____

_____

3. The task force has recommended an early retirement program for all employees

of the company. _____

4. An early retirement program has been recommended for all company employ-

ees. _____

Which voice would you use for:

A notice to all employees of the company announcing a change in retirement benefits?

_____ Voice

Why? _____

_____

5. I urge all company employees to contribute as much as possible to this worthy

cause. _____

6. All company employees are urged to contribute as much as possible to this wor-

thy cause. _____

Which voice would you use for:

A memorandum sent companywide to promote the "worthy cause" and signed by you. (You are probably a high-ranking officer of the corporation.)

_____ Voice

Why? _____

_____

A memorandum sent to members of your team because you've been appointed team chairman of the "worthy cause."

_____ Voice

Why? _____

_____

7. Your tax return must be completed before April 15. _____

8. You must complete your tax return before April 15. _____

Which voice would you use for:

A letter in which this sentence is part of a series of instructions to taxpayers from the IRS specifying procedures and deadlines for the completion of tax returns.

_____ Voice

Why? _____

_____

9. A more concise presentation of ideas needs to be organized for our next mee-

ting. _____

10. Please organize your ideas and present them more concisely at our next meeting. ──────────

Which voice would you use when:

You're the boss writing to a group of your employees. You're trying to get them to be more responsive at meetings without wasting everyone's time by long-winded speeches.

──────────── Voice

Why? ────────────────────────────────

────────────────────────────────

You're an employee with a long-winded boss. In a follow-up report on a meeting you had with him, you're trying to plant the seed of the idea that he needs to be more organized in his meetings with you.

──────────── Voice

Why? ────────────────────────────────

────────────────────────────────

COMMENTARY: ACTIVE OR PASSIVE?

1. Profits were increased by Burco Inc. in 1996. ──── P ────

2. Burco Inc. increased its profits in 1996. ──── A ────

Which voice would you use for:

A report to a current investor thinking of buying Burco stock?

Active Voice

Why? The emphasis in the active sentence is on Burco as the generator of increased profits. Burco's ability to make profits would be of primary interest to someone thinking of investing in the company's stock.

A report to current stockholders?

Passive Voice

Why? Current stockholders have already committed themselves to Burco and are interested in the return they can expect on their investment.

3. The task force has recommended an early retirement program for all employees

of the company. _____A_____

4. An early retirement program has been recommended for all company employ-

ees. _____P_____

Which voice would you use for:

A notice to all employees of the company announcing a change in retirement benefits?

Passive Voice

Why? Employees would be interested in the content of the recommendation, not the group that made it.

5. I urge all company employees to contribute as much as possible to this worthy

cause. _____A_____

6. All company employees are urged to contribute as much as possible to this wor-

thy cause. _____P_____

Which voice would you use for:

A memorandum sent companywide to promote the "worthy cause" and signed by you. (You are probably a high-ranking officer of the corporation.)

Active Voice

Why? You want your name associated with the cause in people's minds. This association is likely to prompt them to contribute.

A memorandum sent to members of your team because you've been appointed team chairman of the "worthy cause."

Passive Voice

Why? Your role as the one urging people to give money does not add additional value to the cause in their minds. In fact, your association with the cause might be negative for some people, who prefer not to be told what charities to give to. You may not want to be thought of as one who tells others where to make charitable contributions.

7. Your tax return must be completed before April 15. _____P_____

8. You must complete your tax return before April 15. _____A_____

Which voice would you use for:

A letter in which this sentence is part of a series of instructions to taxpayers from the IRS specifying procedures and deadlines for the completion of tax returns.

Passive Voice

Why? You want to focus the reader on completing the return before the deadline. The reader may choose to have his or her accountant complete the return. The active statement "You must complete . . . " is therefore misleading.

9. A more concise presentation of ideas needs to be organized for our next meet-

ing. _____P_____

10. Please organize your ideas and present them concisely at our next meeting.

_____A_____

Which voice would you use when:

You're the boss writing to a group of your employees. You're trying to get them to be more responsive at meetings without wasting everyone's time by long-winded speeches.

Active Voice

Why? You're a superior writing to subordinates and, in a polite way, admonishing them to "shape up."

You're an employee with a long-winded boss. In a follow-up report on a meeting you had with him, you're trying to plant the seed of the idea that he needs to be more organized in his meetings with you.

Passive Voice

Why? You're a subordinate writing to a superior. You need to be tactful about pointing out his or her weakness.

CHAPTER 6

Purpose and Vocabulary

Becoming Sensitive to Words
The Problem with Abstract Words

BECOMING SENSITIVE TO WORDS

Here's some good news and some bad news about English. The good news is the English language contains an enormous number of words. It is one of the most expressive vocabularies in the world. The bad news is this richness of opportunity allows so many choices that clarity and tonal appropriateness are often sacrificed for some other intent.

Purpose determines word choice. In polemical writing, the writer intends to argue and persuade. In literary writing, such as a passage in a novel, or a poem, the writer expresses moods, feelings, or other subjective states of mind. In a discussion of physics, the writer explains a highly abstract concept or principle.

In business writing, the purpose is generally clear, direct communication of non-controversial, factual subjects. It is probably closest in purpose and, therefore, in tone and style to expository writing. People may write "I feel" a lot in business, but they're really talking about ideas and facts, not feelings—ideas and facts which are used to explain, inform, and instruct.

Achieving an appropriate tone is just as important in business writing as in other kinds of writing. Tone comes primarily from words. The most basic tool any good writer needs is sensitivity to words.

Sensitivity to words relies on knowing what they mean. Words have two kinds of meanings—denotative and connotative. *Denotation* is the precise meaning a word carries, what you might think of as the dictionary definition. *Connotation* is the feelings and imagery a word evokes, what you might think of as its associated meanings.

For example, all of these words basically mean, or *denote*, the same thing:

- drunk
- intoxicated
- inebriated
- tipsy
- soused

The connotations are different, however. Being *tipsy* is thought of as a milder and more jovial form of drunkenness than being *intoxicated* or *inebriated*. *Drunk* is probably the most neutral and objective term, whereas *soused* carries the connotation of being drunk in a disorderly, falling-down sort of way. It's the connotations of these words that determine how you use them

Some words are used primarily for their denotative meaning, which is precise and specialized: for example, jargon and words derived from Greek, Old French, or Latin roots (see Ch. 7, "Straight Talk," for a discussion of this type of vocabulary). Other words have such abstract meanings that to communicate clearly they must be combined with examples or more concrete vocabulary.

To use any word effectively, you must be sensitive to its strengths and limitations. It all boils down to being interested enough in words themselves to consider why you're making one choice over another.

The most important and easily accessible tool writers have for choosing words appropriately is the dictionary. A good dictionary will define the denotative and, often, the connotative meanings of words. The most fundamental error a writer can make is choosing a word that doesn't mean what he or she thinks it does. The more specialized the word is or the more richly connotative it is, the easier it is to be mistaken about its meaning.

Exercise: Connotation and Denotation

The writers of the following sentences probably failed to check their dictionary. You're going to have the opportunity now to improve their word choice. Read each sentence and explain why the underlined words carry the wrong connotation or denotation for the context. In each case, supply a more appropriate word. If you have problems, by all means use your dictionary.

1. We wanted to have our office party at Gregory's, but our boss <u>negated</u> the idea.

Problem with word choice: ————————————

More appropriate word: ————————————

2. I am pleased with the <u>drastic</u> improvement in your tardiness record over the last few weeks.

Problem with word choice: ————————————

More appropriate word: ————————————

3. Return on sales <u>experienced</u> a considerable increase over the five-year historical period studied.

Problem with word choice: ————————————

More appropriate word: ————————————

4. The company must <u>enhance</u> its sales by opening new retail outlets in areas where it has never done business before.

Problem with word choice: ————————————

More appropriate word: ————————————

5. The new advertising program is <u>merely</u> intended to provide the company with a whole new image.

Problem with word choice: ————————————

More appropriate word: ————————————

6. I would find it <u>pleasurable</u> to be of service to you.

Problem with word choice: ————————————

More appropriate word: ————————————

7. That was a very <u>crafty</u> proposal you made.

Problem with word choice: ————————————————

More appropriate word: ————————————————

8. It was truly a pleasure having my first personal <u>interaction</u> at Largo Company with such an intelligent and dynamic person as you.

Problem with word choice: ————————————————

More appropriate word: ————————————————

SAMPLE REVISIONS: EXERCISE ON CONNOTATION AND DENOTATION

1. We wanted to have our office party at Gregory's, but our boss <u>negated</u> the idea.

   Problem with word choice: Wrong word altogether. <u>Negated</u> means to nullify or deny the truth of.

   More appropriate word: <u>opposed, objected to, rejected</u>

2. I am pleased with the <u>drastic</u> improvement in your tardiness record over the last few weeks.

   Problem with word choice: <u>Drastic</u> means <u>harsh, rigorous,</u> or <u>severe,</u> as in <u>drastic</u> punishment.

   More appropriate word: <u>noticeable</u> or <u>dramatic</u>

3. Return on sales <u>experienced</u> a considerable increase over the five-year historical period studied.

   Problem with word choice: People <u>experience</u> things, but ratios do not.

   More appropriate word: <u>increased, went up</u>

4. The company must <u>enhance</u> sales by opening new retail outlets in areas where it has never done business before.

   Problem with word choice: <u>Enhance</u> means to raise to a higher degree or to raise the value or price of. The sentence seems to be about increasing sales by opening more stores.

   More appropriate word: <u>grow, increase, make more</u>

5. The new advertising program is <u>merely</u> intended to provide the company with a whole new image.

Problem with word choice: <u>Merely</u> means only as specified, and nothing more, as in "merely as a matter of form." The context clearly calls for a different word.

More appropriate word: <u>primarily</u>, <u>mainly</u>, or just eliminate <u>merely</u>

6. I would find it <u>pleasurable</u> to be of service to you.

Problem with word choice: The adjective <u>pleasurable</u> derives from the noun <u>pleasure</u>, which connotes strong physical sensations or strong feelings of joy or delight. All these connotations seem inappropriate for this context.

More appropriate word: <u>enjoyable</u>, <u>be pleased</u>, or <u>be glad</u>

7. That was a very <u>crafty</u> proposal you made.

Problem with word choice: <u>Crafty</u> connotes being shrewd in a <u>deceitful</u> way. (In some cases, of course, this could be the right word.)

More appropriate word: <u>shrewd</u>, <u>clever</u>

8. It was truly a pleasure having my first personal <u>interaction</u> at Largo Company with such an intelligent and dynamic person as you.

Problem with word choice: Interaction means mutual action or influence. It's too abstract for this context.

More appropriate word: <u>meeting</u>, <u>contact</u>, <u>visit</u>

THE PROBLEM WITH ABSTRACT WORDS

Some people find it difficult to be down to earth in their business writing. Their writing is always straining toward the lofty realm of the abstract, just out of reach of the reader's comprehension.

Example: The recession will gain momentum and impact the company's cyclical ventures.

Example: A clear vision as manifested in a direct objective shared by all within an organization is paramount in a dynamic, complex environment.

Example: To the extent that an entity does not affect the dynamics of its environment, the appropriate response to change will necessarily be dictated by the environment. The essence of operating in a complex marketplace is not to adapt but rather to become adaptable on an ongoing basis.

Most people speak easily in direct, concrete terms and examples. In general, we think in concrete particulars more easily than in abstract ideas. After all, our everyday lives are made up of millions of concrete actions—buying the newspaper, opening the front door, cooking dinner, and so on.

Thus the tendency to write abstractly is not the result of a primary tendency to speak and think this way. Yet when people put their thoughts on paper, abstractions often abound.

There are basically two motivations behind a tendency to favor abstract words in writing. One is a conscious motive. People want to be precise rather than misleading. When trying to be precise, people are often "all-inclusive." This means they attempt to define the total universe in which something might take place.

For example, consider the sentence "We are taking precautions against fire." The word *precautions* is all-inclusive. It may be used to indicate many things that are being done. It may be used to indicate some things that are being done and others that will be done (but are not yet known). But the word does not define *exactly* what will be done—it gives only a general idea of the total universe of possible fire precautions. However, if you write "We are installing fire doors and an automatic sprinkler system," the reader knows precisely what will be done.

In addition, defining the total universe of something suggests theoretical discourse to many people. Explaining theories requires abstract vocabulary because these words are necessary to elucidate the world of ideas. But little of what is written in the everyday world of business really qualifies as "theoretical."

A second motive—a less conscious one—stems from self-preservation. Whenever people put things on paper, they know what is written is going to last. Unlike spoken words, which have a life of a brief moment and can be changed by simply saying, "What I said was" or "That's not what I said," written words are not as easily erased. In particular, business writers, who are anticipating a response from their readers, consider what reactions and attacks may be engendered by their writing.

These "attacks" can come in different forms:

- "Why didn't you . . . "
- "Did you investigate . . . "
- "Did you think of . . . "
- "What about . . . "

A sinking feeling comes over most business writers when they contemplate such responses.

Fear of such responses is not a case of paranoia. It is based in reality. History provides a lengthy record of attacks on people's writings and the consequences suffered by the writers. One can think of many examples: Martin Luther when he nailed the 95 theses to the church door, Galileo's revolutionary theories, and Freud's case studies.

Think back to many of your college and high school courses. Didn't they often include a critique of someone's ideas through his or her writing? And of course, receiving a grade on a written paper or examination always meant receiving a critique of your own written ideas.

The way to protect oneself from a professor's critique, as most students readily learn, is to become more abstract and, therefore, harder to pin down on any specific points (or potential errors).

This self-protective mechanism works for self-protection. It does not, however, aid clear communication. Self-protection must ultimately be sacrificed if you want to be clear about communicating what you think. Martin Luther, Galileo, and Freud knew this and undoubtedly braced themselves for the consequences. But they were more anxious to communicate a new idea to the world than to protect themselves.

I doubt that any of you will be called upon to die for your ideas. Yet everyone knows that the power of the written word is enormous. These subliminal realizations often call up business writers' protective mechanisms when they must go "on the record."

Let's consider again the example, "We are taking precautions against fire." If somebody writes specifically, "We are installing fire doors and an automatic sprinkler system," the writer may be concerned that somebody else will say, "And what about smoke detectors?" So he or she writes instead, "We are taking precautions against fire."

Not only do people fear attack from those who disagree with them. What about those who are sympathetic? How many people fear the so-called well-meaning criticism of friends, bosses, and teachers, playing devil's advocate against their ideas. There's a trite but true saying: With friends like this, who needs enemies?

In no way, of course, am I implying that you should, could, or would want to write without abstract words. But you must combine them properly with concrete words and examples.

Definitions are a precise blend of the abstract and the concrete. Think for a moment about how you might define a pen. Some of the phrases that may come to mind are

- my pen is blue
- long, thin instrument
- writing instrument

- uses ink
- ballpoint or fountain

Of course, all of these can be challenged. *Long* and *thin* could also describe a toothbrush. A writing instrument could be a pencil. A rubber stamp uses ink. Pencils can be blue. "Ballpoint" or "fountain" describes specific types of pens.

As you may have already guessed, part of defining something is to put it into an abstract category: A pen is a *writing instrument*. But this alone does not define a pen. The description must also be concrete: A pen is a *long, thin* writing instrument that *uses ink*. Combining the abstract category and specific descriptions yields a satisfying definition of a pen.

Thus the issue in good writing, especially in business writing, is achieving the needed balance between abstract words and concrete words, using examples to communicate points clearly and completely.

I am assuming that your objective in business writing generally will *not* be to be purposefully unclear. Writers and speakers who purposely obfuscate have basically dishonest motives behind the profusion of abstract words that they throw at the reader or listener. I can only deal with the motivations I've already discussed, which are basically honest, though not always necessary.

Exercise: Blending Abstract and Concrete

Blending the abstract and the concrete requires three kinds of knowledge:

- of your subject
- of your message
- of words.

Not all abstract words should be eliminated. But if a passage has too many abstract terms at the expense of concrete words and examples, the readers may not understand the message, may not interpret it correctly, or may simply "turn off."

Each of the following three paragraphs is about a different topic: buying a car, gardening, and music.

Pick the paragraph that interests you most. Then list the abstract words in the spaces provided.

Buying a Car

It is important to be aware of quality when choosing a personal vehicle. A vehicle is seen as most valuable when it reflects lifestyle and personality. Reliability, maintenance, and dependability are also considered significant factors.

List all of the abstract words you can find in this paragraph.

_____

_____

_____

_____

_____

_____

_____

The Joys of Gardening

Gardening is a very satisfying activity. The most enjoyable part is the maintenance of the garden. The physical activity required is very healthy. It's also invigorating to be out of doors and experience your environment.

List all of the abstract words you can find in this paragraph.

_____

_____

_____

_____

_____

_____

Listening to Music

People generally listen to music that they think expresses their personality. Thus some people like rock, some like jazz, and some like classical. There are vastly different moods and world views embodied in these three styles. Some people think each of these types of music speaks a different language to the listener.

List all of the abstract words you can find in this paragraph.

_____

_____

_____

_____

_____

_____

Here is a list of the abstract words.

Buying a Car

quality, vehicle, valuable, reflects, lifestyle, personality, reliability, maintenance, dependability, significant factors

The Joys of Gardening

activity, maintenance, physical activity, healthy, experience, environment

Listening to Music

expresses, personality, rock, jazz, classical, moods, world views, embodied, styles, types, language

Once again, choose one of the three paragraphs that interests you most. Then, for the underlined abstract words, substitute words or examples that would, in the context, make the writing more concrete. (You may, of course, revise all three paragraphs.)

Using an example from <u>Buying a Car</u>, here's how I would make the abstraction, <u>lifestyle</u>, more concrete.

> People who think of themselves as "success stories" but also "free sprits" often drive sports cars as part of their lifestyle. The moderately wealthy adventurer might choose a Corvette or perhaps a Firebird. But for most people I know, the symbol of total success and total freedom remains the Porsche.

I substituted words and examples that come from my experience of buying a car. Your revision will come from your experience.

Rewrite the underlined abstractions in the paragraph of your choice.

Buying a Car

It is important to be aware of quality when choosing a personal vehicle. A vehicle is seen as most valuable when it reflects lifestyle and personality. Reliability, maintenance, and dependability are also considered significant factors.

Your revision

_____

_____

_____

_____

_____

The Joys of Gardening

Gardening is a very satisfying activity. The most enjoyable part is the maintenance of the garden. The physical activity required is very healthy. It's also invigorating to be out of doors and experience your environment.

Your revision

_____

_____

_____

_____

_____

Listening to Music

People generally listen to music that they think expresses their personality. Thus some people like rock, some like jazz, and some like classical. There are vastly different <u>moods</u> and world views <u>embodied</u> in these three styles. Some people think each of these types of music speaks a different <u>language</u> to the listener.

Your revision

_____

_____

_____

_____

_____

COMMENTARY: BLENDING ABSTRACT AND CONCRETE

Here are some sample revisions. Yours will undoubtedly be different and may be better. Make sure you have a good blend of the abstract and the concrete.

Buying a Car

It is important to be aware of quality when choosing a personal vehicle. Whether it's a jeep, moped, skateboard, or Ferrari, you don't want it to break down and leave you stranded on a dark road at night. You also want your vehicle to express your personality. The free spirits who like the wind in their hair prefer the free-wheeling style of a convertible. After all, aren't skateboards and mopeds just a form of convertible?

The Joys of Gardening

Gardening is very satisfying to the senses. When you hoe the earth to prepare it to receive seeds or bulbs, you touch it, smell it, and feel it. It's invigorating to smell clay and lime. Dig deeper and you may feel the slimy touch of an earthworm before you see its almost transparent form blending with the earth. The final sensory pleasure is the vibrant gold of a jonquil bed or the piquant taste of a radish.

Listening to Music

People generally listen to the music they believe expresses their personality. Lovers of order and structure may enjoy the music of classical composers such as Mozart and Haydn, whereas emotional, expressive people may prefer music by Brahms and Berlioz. The terms _classicist_ and _romantic_ are often used to distinguish the different sensibilities of these personality types.

CHAPTER 7

Straight Talk

"Elegant" Words
"Elegant" Phrases
Is Jargon Good or Bad?

"ELEGANT" WORDS

When William the Conqueror conquered England in 1066, the English language was changed forever. For generations after the Norman Conquest, the most important political and social positions in England were held by French-speaking Normans. Writing, which was usually done by clergy, was done in Latin. And the "people" spoke old English ("Englisc"), a fusion of Saxon, Viking, and Danish languages.

Old English reflected the everyday life of an agricultural people. Our modern English is impossible without this vocabulary. Computer analysis has shown that the one hundred most common words in English—words such as *the, you, what, that*—are Anglo-Saxon.[1]

The aristocrats carried on the "higher" activities of society—religion, law, science, and literature—in French or Latin. Latin was primarily the language of religion and learning, whereas French was spoken in "high society."

From the mingling of these three languages—Old English, Latin, and French—modern English developed its enormous vocabulary and its ability to express shades of meaning and fine distinctions.

The mingling of these three powerful traditions can be seen in the case of a word like *kingly.* The Anglo-Saxons had only one word to express this concept, which, with typi-

[1]Robert McCrum, William Cran, and Robert MacNeil, *The Story of English* (New York: Elisabeth Sifton Books, Viking, 1986), p. 61.

cal simplicity, they made up from the word king. After the Normans, three synonyms enter the language: *royal, regal,* and *sovereign.*[2]

As the language developed, the simple, concrete activities of the "people" (who were usually serfs) survived in the large Anglo-Saxon vocabulary that provides the building blocks of the language. The words used for finer, more abstract concepts and distinctions usually find their roots in Latin or sometimes French.

The problem we have in business writing is not whether to use Anglo-Saxon words or the language of the aristocracy. Rather, the issue is how to choose the appropriate word for the purpose of clear communication and tonal rightness.

Latinate words such as *ameliorate, edification,* and *disseminate* have precise meanings and are used to express nuances within a context. Anglo-Saxon words such as *kick, walk,* and *work* are the vocabulary of common parlance. Times haven't changed so much.

When writers use Latinate vocabulary for the purpose of impressing rather than for the purpose of precision, the words are often misused.

Consider these two sentences:

1. The following progress report is presented for your *edification.* (Latin root)
2. This progress report will tell you *what has been done.* (Anglo-Saxon)

What does the word *edification* mean? According to Webster's it means the "act of instructing or improving, especially in moral and religious knowledge." Thinking back to the use of Latin as the language of the church, we can understand better its root meaning. *Edification* really has a very narrow meaning. A progress report written in a business situation is unlikely to *edify* anyone.

The point is that often Latin-based words are actually misused by writers seeking to impress the reader with the sight and sound of an expanded vocabulary. The lack of familiarity of these words probably means most people won't understand them when they first read them. A word like *edification* as used in this sentence actually miscommunicates, because it doesn't mean what the writer thinks it does.

Thus before you use a Latinate word or some other "unfamiliar" word in common parlance, *make sure it means what you think it does.* And given the precision of context necessary for Latinate words, you'll probably find yourself returning to everyday Anglo-Saxon for most business writing. After all, business is mostly concrete actions. Religion, science, literature, and even law are not the stuff of the everyday business world.

However, if your context requires a precise meaning found in Latinate vocabulary, then by all means use it. Sometimes your context can simply be enriched or made

[2]McCrum et al., p. 75.

more precise by the *proper* use of Latinate words. That is your judgment. Part of developing stylistic flexibility is the ability to set standards appropriate to the occasion and the reader. Keep in mind that misuse of a Latinate word will *not* enrich the context or stimulate the reader.

Here is a list of Latin or Old French-derived words with some simpler equivalents. Ask yourself before using them, Do I really need to use this word? Is it precisely what my context calls for?

Why say	If it's clearer or more correct to say	
abate	decrease	reduce
accumulate	gather	collect
acquiesce	agree	go along with
additional	added	more
ameliorate	improve	make better
approximately	about	almost
circumvent	avoid	get around
disseminate	distribute	disperse
endeavor	try	attempt
forfeit	give up	lose
initiate	start	begin
instance	case	example
minimal	least	smallest
numerous	a lot	many
obviate	get around	prevent
optimum	best	foremost
reciprocate	give in return	give back
rectify	correct	improve
require	need	want
rescind	take back	call off
simplistic	simple	easy
solicit	seek	ask for
verify	confirm	find out the truth of

"ELEGANT" PHRASES

Along with Latinate vocabulary, business writers often use wordy, old-fashioned phrases that mar their writing. They seem to think these phrases make their writing sound more elegant.

Again, there is a historical precedent for this stylistic concept. Since the Renaissance, English writers have revered the classics. They embellished their prose with Latinate words and, to some degree, mirrored the syntax of the Latin language. At the same time, a debate emerged and has been raging ever since over "elegant" writing versus "plain" style.

Shakespeare summarized the debate with a typically striking phrase. When Berowne finally declares his love for Rosaline in *Love's Labour's Lost* he announces that he will shun "taffeta phrases, silken terms precise." Instead

> . . . my wooing mind shall be express'd
> In russet yeas and honest kersey noes.[3]

Business writers, whether knowingly or unknowingly, have inherited this tradition. How many times have I heard business people in a writing class say, "That sentence flows well" or "That sentence just sounds abrupt to me if you take all those words out."

The desire to round out a sentence or to make it flow is not bad. This is the elegance English prose stylists have always sought. You must develop a fine ear, however, to avoid excesses or the mere imitation of a stylistic concept that should be assessed *first* for its usefulness to a modern business person and *second* for its very beauty.

Many modern business writers aspire to elegance and a very formal style in their writing. They try to achieve this quality by embellishing their writing with

- Latinate vocabulary
- "Elegant" phrases

Consider these examples from real business reports which show one or both of these stylistic tendencies.

1. Due to the fact that we live in litigious times, it is not seemly for management to act in any way that might promote problematical dealings with respect to potential marketing prospects.

2. We need to formulate an approach to define for us those messages and attitudes optimal for our work environment in order that we may better manage them toward desired results.

3. It is a matter of regret, therefore, that this report on the subject seems so unpromising and that because of this your request for specific recommendations cannot be complied with.

4. If any further information pertaining to this subject is required, do not hesitate to get in touch with me at your convenience.

The style of these examples is not really elegant. Certainly, it is not direct and clear.

George Orwell said it best about prose style, I think, in his classic essay, "Politics and the English Language." He lays down five rules of thumb that cover what I've been saying to you for the last eighty-odd pages. Then he adds, "Break any of these rules sooner than say anything outright barbarous."[4]

---

[3]McCrum et al., pp. 95–96.

[4]George Orwell, "Politics and the English Language," reprinted in *A Collection of Essays by George Orwell* (New York: Harcourt Brace Jovanovich, Harbrace Paperbound Library, 1956), p. 170.

Language has rhythm and sound. The rhythms of English are a blend of many tonalities. Thus you must develop and use your ear. Read your prose aloud. You'll find yourself naturally avoiding awkward phrasing and stylistic ugliness.

Here's a partial list of elegant phrases with plain equivalents. There are many, many more. Elegant phrases can destroy the flow and rhythm of a sentence and thus its readability. Good writers train their ears to listen carefully for the intrusive rhythms of these phrases.

Elegant phrase	Plain style
Acknowledge receipt of	Thank you for your . . .
	I (or we) have received . . .
Along the lines of	like
As per your request	According to (or simply state your reply to the request)
Arrived at the conclusion that	concluded or decided
Due to the fact that	since, because
In accordance with your request	as you asked
Inasmuch as	since
In the amount of	for
In the event that	if
In this connection	(omit the phrase)
Prior to	before
Subsequent to	after
Upon receipt of	When we receive
Until such time as	until
We regret to inform you	We are sorry
With the exception of	except
With reference to	about

Exercise and Suggested Revisions: Revising "Elegant" Style

Excessive use of Latinate vocabulary and elegant phrasing is not a natural style of speaking or writing today. People who write for business in an excessively elegant way had to *learn* this style of writing. They learned it by imitation and by receiving approval from others who wrote in this way. This style is one type of bureaucratic writing or "officialese" that spreads in some business environments.

Now let's reverse this process of imitation.

First, you'll have the opportunity to read two sentences and change the language. Your goal is to make the style simpler and more direct, the way a modern business person would be most likely to speak.

After you've revised these two sentences, compare your answers to the suggested revisions. Then you'll revise two more sentences, look at the revisions, two more sentences, and then another two, until you've finally worked through eight revisions. Through this process of revising and checking your revisions, you can become more sensitive to these kinds of problems and develop your ear to hear a simpler, more direct style. As we discussed earlier, part of the problem with changing habits of elegant writing is that many people have gotten used to and have even come to approve of the rhythm and vocabulary of this kind of writing.

You may want to refer to the lists of Latinate words (p. 123) and "elegant" phrases (p. 125) for ideas to use in your revisions. Be sure to revise all of the sentences.

Rewrite these sentences. Simplify the language and make them more direct.

1. As agreed upon in our meeting of February 28, to assist us in conducting the office equipment inventory, it will be necessary to obtain the services of two "volunteers" on a full-time basis from each department.

Your revision

_____

_____

2. Viewing the program objectively, it could be said that there are various deficiencies which might in future years lead to ramifications such as diminution of earnings.

Your revision

_____

_____

Compare your revisions with these. Once again, do not look at the revisions as the "right" answer. Rather, use them as a guide to evaluate your own work. Which do you like better? Why?

1. We need two full-time "volunteers" from each department to help us conduct the office equipment inventory.

(**Note:** If you think it's important to remind the reader of the February 28 meeting, the sentence can begin, "As we agreed on February 28, we need. . . .")

2. The program has problems that could lead to reduced earnings.

Make these sentences simpler and more direct.

3. As you know, the procedure for 1997 will be substantially the same as in 1996, but it will still be necessary to disseminate the procedure to the Personnel Administrators for distribution to the appropriate personnel in their departments.

Your revision

_____

_____

4. Members of the task force are at variance with each other regarding an expeditious solution to the conflict.

Your revision

_____

_____

Here are some possible revisions.

3. We must send the 1997 version of the procedure to the Personnel Administrators. They should then give their people copies of it.

4. The task force members cannot agree on an easy way to settle the conflict.

Make these sentences simpler and more direct.

5. We acknowledge receipt of your letter of recent date advising us of your new address.

Your revision

_____

_____

6. It might be well if the urgency of this situation could be brought to the attention of the departments by means of a memo from us.

Your revision

_____

_____

Here are some possible revisions.

5. We have received your new address.

6. We need to send the departments a memo telling them the problem.

Make these sentences simpler and more direct.

7. I have drafted a possible finalized version of the procedure and it is herewith attached for your perusal.

Your revision

_____

_____

8. The investigation was carried out by the Auditing Department for the purpose of determining the accuracy of the financial statements submitted by us.

Your revision

_____

_____

Here are some possible revisions.

7. A possible final draft of the procedure is attached for you to read.

8. The Auditing Department has investigated the financial statements we submitted.

IS JARGON GOOD OR BAD?

Jargon means _technical language._ It provides a useful medium of communication for people who understand it and is meaningless to everybody else.

Here's an excerpt from a letter by a Marketing Support Analyst working for a major computer company. He's writing to another systems employee:

> The Operating System 16.7 will introduce EPFs. This enables runtime code to page into memory directly, bypassing the usage of the paging disk. EPF programs may call other programs (not just subroutines) and will utilize the new BIND utility instead of the SEG-LOADER. Execution time will therefore be greatly enhanced . . . This revision will also permit the automatic detection of asynchronous baud rate through use of new config directive "ASD."

Although this may be "Greek" to most of us, it's perfectly clear to them.

Suppose, however, a physician and patient were to have the following conversation:

Doctor: You have a severe hematoma as a result of your accident. Related stress and anxiety have produced chronic spasms of the duodenum.

Patient: Huh?

Doctor: You have a bad bruise and recurring stomach aches that are probably coming from stress.

Most of us would probably agree that this doctor's bedside manner was lacking. Would most patients know what he's saying? This is an inappropriate use of jargon.

Technicians who use jargon when speaking or writing may do so for good reasons.

- They want to communicate with another technician.
- They want to indicate their membership in a profession, trade, business, or some other sort of specialized fraternity.

In these situations, if you truly "know your stuff," your language signals this to the group members and you're accepted. If the language is imprecisely or incorrectly used, you're marked and excluded.

When speaking or writing to a layperson, however, as in the case of doctor and patient, people's motives for using jargon may be less laudable. For example:

- They want to impress people with their technical status.
- They do not understand their technical world well enough to express it in plain English.

Because we live in a world that confers status on people who are professionals or technicians, it's easy to see how anyone might want to parade his or her background. If, however, technicians commit themselves to explaining something technical to nontechnical readers, they must take the time to define or give examples of terms and concepts unknown to laypeople.

In short, the degree to which you should use jargon depends on *your audience*. An appropriate and good use of jargon is when two scientists, physicians, computer technicians, or other technical specialists are using the language to achieve precision in their communication. Jargon is a kind of shorthand for these people. It would take many more words to say what they mean without jargon.

An inappropriate and perhaps even unethical use of jargon is when a contractor of some kind uses jargon to impress or to sell something to a potential client who really does not understand the specialized language.

When jargon becomes trendy, it often graduates to the status of a *buzzword*. Buzzwords are specious jargon. Their denotative meanings, and thus their technical precision, are lost. Only the glamour of the worlds they came from remains. For example:

- Once the departments have *interfaced,* their *outputs* should improve considerably.

These terms, which have technical meanings in the computer world, are vague in this context. But they're still trailing their high-tech aura. Since the writer is apparently talking about improving efficiency, she chose the words more for their suggestive qualities than for their meaning.

All disciplines, of course, have their jargon to a greater or lesser extent. Yet jargon, even for the technical reader, can be taken to excess. The degree to which jargon or buzzwords may have permeated your style in a detrimental way is a judgment you must make each time you write. Part of your judgment will hinge on for whom you're writing and what you're writing about. Part will hinge on what your "ear" tells you will be readable or not.

Here's an example of what one bank vice president's ear told him was an excessive use of jargon:

> Company X's asset conversion cycle demands a heavy mix of illiquid assets; further, the industry is subject to definite cyclicality of demand. Having financed its latest growth curve with debt, the company appears to no longer be a viable credit risk. Its ROE makes it an unattractive capital investment, yet its ROS and ALEV are more appropriate to a low value-added operation and its debt-to-worth ratio is more appropriate to a dealer in hedgeable commodities than a capital- and labor-intensive manufacturer in a basic industry. A quick and dirty analysis of its current or working asset quality reveals a working capital inadequacy and an inability to clean up senior liabilities in a high point liquidation even if we were protected by the seniority afforded by a perfected floating lien on all personal assets.

As you've probably realized, I am using *ear* as a metaphor for an aesthetic sense or standard of good writing. I use "good writing" to encompass such connotations as *clear, direct, communicative,* and, yes, sometimes even *beautiful.* All good writers are continually developing this inner ear. And if it's really developing, it will remain susceptible to change.

To help you become more sensitive to jargon and buzzwords, the table on page 131 entitled "Types of Jargon" lists some common terms and the specialized worlds they come from. A list of common buzzwords is also provided.

Exercise: Jargon and Buzzwords

Revise these sentences so that the message is expressed in simpler, less technical terms by

- eliminating unclear jargon or buzzwords; and
- adding, deleting, or rearranging parts of the sentence to achieve clarity.

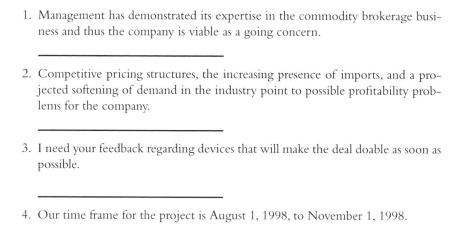

1. Management has demonstrated its expertise in the commodity brokerage business and thus the company is viable as a going concern.

2. Competitive pricing structures, the increasing presence of imports, and a projected softening of demand in the industry point to possible profitability problems for the company.

3. I need your feedback regarding devices that will make the deal doable as soon as possible.

4. Our time frame for the project is August 1, 1998, to November 1, 1998.

5. Further improvement of sales is expected as the company focuses on Third World nations which need heavy machinery to build their infrastructure and as the company also continues its emphasis on new product development and the enhancement of sales techniques in its dealer network.

SUGGESTED REVISIONS: EXERCISE ON JARGON AND BUZZWORDS

Once again, remember that these are only suggested responses. Yours will undoubtedly be different and may be better.

1. The company is likely to remain in business because skillful commodity brokers manage it.

2. Competitive prices, more imports, and less demand for its products may decrease the company's profits.

3. I need your thoughts about ways to do the deal as soon as possible.

4. The project will begin August 1, 1998, and end by November 1, 1998.

5. The company expects to sell a lot of heavy machinery to developing countries, create new products, and improve the salesmanship of its dealers.

Note: You could keep *Third World* or use *underdeveloped*, though the connotations of these terms have become more and more negative. *Developing* is also economics jargon but carries a more positive connotation.

Types of Jargon

Legal Jargon	Accounting Jargon	Economics Jargon	Financial Jargon	Computer Jargon	Specious Jargon or Buzzwords
subordinated debt	balance sheet	infrastructure	tenor	boot up	ultimate
secured basis	income statement	integration a) vertical b) horizontal	mitigate	log on	expertise
attach	liquidity	capital-intensive	portfolio	bytes	impact (verb)
perfect	liability	labor-intensive	asset protection	megabytes	transact
priority	factoring	Third World	seasonality	data base	institute (verb)
guarantee	fixed or intangible assets	diversified	lead bank	menu	device
lien	plant	cyclicality	run-offs	command	element
floating lien	credit cycle	elastic	projections	hard disk	factor
personal assets	working capital	demand	squeeze	floppy disk	viable
real property	revenue	underdeveloped	leverage	hardware	demonstrate
seniority	expense		cushion	software	experience (verb)
	debit		monitor	window	enhance
	encumbrance		bridge financing	cursor	prioritize
	accounts receivable		profitability	memory	logistical
	accounts payable		going concern	hard drive	time frame
	long-term		"attractive client"	daisy wheel printer	responsive
	short-term		lending vehicle	dot matrix printer	output
	in the red		revolver	laser printer	input
	in the black		participation		feedback
	expenditure		classified loan		per
					parameters
					management
					doable
					focus (verb)
					key (adjective)

CHAPTER 8

Tone

The Components of Tone
Two Categories of Message in Business Writing
Language and Tone
Stating Bad News Tactfully

THE COMPONENTS OF TONE

Good business letters and memoranda succeed in three main ways.

1. **They state the writer's primary goal.** Some typical goals of business letters and memoranda are

   - Asking for information
   - Answering questions
   - Apologizing
   - Asking for action
   - Answering a complaint
   - Soliciting business
   - Solving a problem
   - Issuing a warning

2. **They communicate their message clearly.** Thus the style of the letter or memo is readable and literate. The message is stated in grammatical English, the words chosen are appropriate for the reader and correctly spelled, and the sentences are coherent.

3. **They build goodwill, or, in some cases, retain it.** The writer takes into account the reader's *feelings* as well as the message the letter or memo conveys. When choosing an organizational strategy and the

wording of the message, the writer seeks to create a **tone** that will be appropriate to the particular reader and the situation prompting the letter or memo.

Tone is the aspect of writing that is not necessarily accomplished merely by identifying your purpose and communicating it clearly. Tone might be defined as the "secondary message" of writing—an attitude or idea the reader can identify and articulate along with the primary message. Although not overt, this secondary message is nevertheless immediately apparent to readers. A writer must ensure that it does not obscure or, worse, overshadow the primary message. If it does, the reader may not heed the primary message.

You might reasonably ask, How can an implied message or attitude predominate over the primary message, especially if the primary message is clearly stated? The answer, once again, has to do with the *impact* of the writing. If the impact of the secondary message resonates more strongly with readers than the primary message, then they will pay the most attention to the secondary message.

Business memoranda and, especially, business letters are perceived by recipients as a "personal visitor" into their private world. As a result, tone is an especially important element contributing to the successful delivery of the message. Letters and memos seek to build goodwill or retain it. The writer must take into account the reader's feelings as well as the message the document delivers.

Tone, like body language, is something people immediately recognize and respond to, usually because it touches them more emotionally than intellectually. Writers must recognize and adjust the tone of their writing to ensure that it *aids* the communication of their primary message.

Because tone is easier to recognize than to describe in the abstract, you are going to have the opportunity to identify this "secondary message" as it presents itself in some business writing examples. You will also decide whether you think this message aids or obstructs the central message the writer is trying to communicate.

Exercise: Responding to the Impact of Tone

Put yourself in the reader's place as you read five examples of real business letters. The examples are followed by a "goodwill scale." After you've read an example, circle one of the four descriptions that best describes your reaction to its tone. Then on the line labeled "Secondary Message," state your interpretation of the unspoken or implied message in the example.

Sample #1

Mr. Mark Gooding

12 Garden Drive

San Francisco, CA 98076

Dear Mr. Gooding:

Pursuant to your recent letter concerning overdraft charges on your joint checking account with Mrs. Gladys Gooding, I regret to inform you that we can in no way overlook these charges. This account has a frequent history of overdrawn funds which cause substantial inconvenience, not to mention expense, to this financial institution. May I suggest that you and your wife keep a closer reckoning of your account balance to avoid these charges in the future.

Thank you for banking at Jumbo Bank and we trust that we can continue to satisfy your banking requirements.

Very truly yours,

Karla Smith

Assistant Branch Manager

   (A)   Tone would maintain and add to goodwill

   (B)   Tone would maintain goodwill

   (C)   Tone would damage goodwill

   (D)   Tone would lose goodwill

Secondary Message _____

Sample #2

Ms. Marilyn Jones

55 Apple Street

Madison, Wisconsin 90876

Dear Ms. Jones:

Enclosed are two new Typograph typewriter ribbons for your use. They have been inspected and approved by our Quality Control Department and I assure you that they are of the highest quality and dependability.

The product you had problems with is one of our most reliable and we seldom get complaints about it. However, due to human error, a batch will sometimes escape the attention of our inspectors or assembly persons and then an unfortunate incident, such as what happened to you, will occur.

We, at Typograph, apologize for any inconvenience caused you by our ribbons and we sincerely hope you continue to use the Typograph line of products.

Sincerely yours,

Janice Gibbons

Quality Engineer

    (A)   Tone would maintain and add to goodwill

    (B)   Tone would maintain goodwill

    (C)   Tone would damage goodwill

    (D)   Tone would lose goodwill

Secondary Message _____

Sample #3

Mr. James M. Stetson

1457 Lawson Place

Haddonfield, New Jersey 09876

Dear Mr. Stetson:

We have today closed your account and request that no further deposits be made as they will not be accepted.

Sincerely yours,

Jack Foster

Assistant Vice President

Garden State Bank

    (A)   Tone would maintain and add to goodwill

    (B)   Tone would maintain goodwill

    (C)   Tone would damage goodwill

    (D)   Tone would lose goodwill

Secondary Message _____

Sample #4

Ms. Angela Lands

47 Willow Street

New York, N.Y. 10897

Dear Ms. Lands:

A Selection Committee has reviewed your candidacy for the position of Testing Assessment Specialist in the office of WED Testing Service for the American Education Group.

While the Committee recognizes the accomplishments prompting your candidacy, the applicants whose qualifications more closely meet the selection criteria for the position are now being considered. Your name has, therefore, been removed from our candidate list.

I wish to express our appreciation for your interest in the position and the work of the Group.

Sincerely yours,

Glen Rose

Assistant Director

    (A)   Tone would maintain and add to goodwill

    (B)   Tone would maintain goodwill

    (C)   Tone would damage goodwill

    (D)   Tone would lose goodwill

Secondary Message _____

Sample #5

Dr. Jane M. Leeds

34 Simpson Street

New York, N.Y. 09876

Dear Dr. Leeds:

I am pleased to announce that Glenn Gross, former Marketing Manager of Educational Services for Marketing Resources Group of Delaware, has been appointed

Director of Continuing Education at Jumbo Insurance Company and will begin his work here on March 1, 1995. Mr. Gross's extensive corporate experience in continuing education includes the planning and conducting of 180 seminars in the U.S. and in Europe.

While you were not selected for this position, I wish to express my sincere thanks to you for your interest in our company. I wish you every success in your future endeavors.

Sincerely yours,

J.J. Thomas

Vice President

    (A) Tone would maintain and add to goodwill

    (B) Tone would maintain goodwill

    (C) Tone would damage goodwill

    (D) Tone would lose goodwill

Secondary Message _____

COMMENTARY: RESPONDING TO THE IMPACT OF TONE

Example 1

Most readers of this example in my classes have scored it (C) or (D). Here are some statements they gave of its "secondary message."

- "We aren't interested in your business unless you and your wife can become more organized."
- "Your business is more trouble than it's worth."

Example 2

Most readers of this example in my classes have scored it (A) or (B). They basically articulate the secondary message as follows.

- "We acknowledge our mistake—the product was defective."

However, some readers have scored it (C) because of another secondary message they perceived.

- "We only acknowledge the *possibility* of a mistake ('due to human error'), but we'll take your word for it. Therefore, we're sending you another of our ribbons, which are seldom defective."

These readers disliked the company's seeming rationalization of the defective ribbon. However, most readers have appreciated the gesture of replacing the defective ribbon—an action, they noted, that speaks louder than any "message."

Example 3

Most readers have scored it (D) or E). Some of their interpretations of the secondary message were

- "You are not the kind of customer we want."
- "You are being penalized for overdrawing your account" (or some other bad behavior).

Many students have asked why the bank decided to close the account. Most are surprised to hear that the letter was sent to *confirm the customer's request to close the account*. In this case, a reader expects a confirmation with a "resell" aspect—a statement that the bank appreciates the customer's business or some other strategy for inviting the customer back. When tone violates readers' expectations of "how they should be treated," goodwill is frequently damaged.

When I discuss this letter with my classes, they are always curious about how I got it. It was sent to me by an elderly relative who received it from his local bank when he closed his account. He was so offended that he described it as "being treated like a criminal" and sent it to me cross-country so that I could show it in my classes "as a bad example all business people could learn from."

I am sharing the actual history of this letter because it reminds us that people have feelings. I am pretty sure that the writer did not intend to offend the reader. Probably, this was a reply dashed off in haste and based on the assumption that "the reader knows why I am writing." But the letter did not match a customer's idea of how he should be treated in this situation—nor has it matched the expectations of others who have read it.

My classes note when we read this letter that it actually matches many of the other standards we have been discussing. It is concise. Its primary message—"we are closing your account"—is clearly stated. Yet its tone is problematic. Perhaps adding "As you requested" at the front of the sentence would have clarified its primary message, but I doubt if even this would greatly have changed the letter's impact on a customer who expected that a little more time be taken with him and his account.

Example 4

Readers' scores have ranged from (B) to (D).

Secondary message:

- "You are being crossed off our list completely." (Some people have disliked the mental picture they draw from the sentence "Your name has, therefore, been removed from our candidate list.")
- You're "not quite our kind, dear."

Most people, however, agree that the letter "lets you down slowly," a strategy they expect when they receive bad news.

Example 5

Most readers score it (C) or (D).

Secondary message:

- "We're really tickled we got Glenn Gross for this job. By the way, sorry you didn't get it."

Most people who have read this agree that praising the successful job applicant in a letter intended to inform the unsuccessful applicants is, at best, a confusing and seemingly insensitive strategy.

TWO CATEGORIES OF MESSAGE
IN BUSINESS WRITING

The primary message of most business writing will fall into one of two categories:

Good news or neutral message. For example: granting a request, agreeing to do something, forwarding information, acknowledging receipt or notice of something, answering questions, solving problems, asking for information.

Bad news or negative message. For example: warning the reader, turning down requests or applications, threatening the reader.

To make sure that your tone will match your readers' expectations of how they should be addressed, you will need to decide *which type of primary message you are delivering.* Then you can more easily inspect your writing to decide whether your strategy and language deliver the message appropriately and sensitively.

ORGANIZING GOOD NEWS OR NEUTRAL MESSAGES

When the message of a letter or memo is neutral or good news, you state the main points at the beginning, usually in the first paragraph, and then explain the reasons or details for those main points in the body of the writing.

This strategy, as you now know, is called most important to least important order. Business readers prefer it because it is easy to read. The most important points are clearly stated at the beginning and less important evidence or details are relegated to minor positions in the body. Busy readers may not choose to read the entire document, but this kind of organization ensures that they will be able to learn the important points—that is, the "good news"—right away.

The good news letter is a classic example of most important to least important order. Here again is the diagram of this pattern.

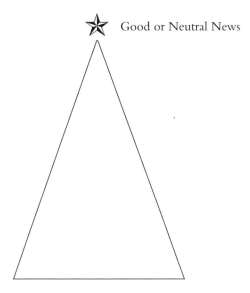 Good or Neutral News

The key idea is to give readers what they want to know right away. When there is nothing for them to respond unfavorably to, why delay the message?

ORGANIZING THE BAD NEWS MESSAGE

When the message of a memo or letter is bad news, you should consider using a different form of organization from most important to least important order.

The bad news form is just the opposite of the good news form. Because the reader may respond negatively to the message, you may decide to *delay* presentation of the main points to gain your reader's acceptance of the message.

Rejecting a person's job application or criticizing aspects of a person's performance in a job appraisal are times when you probably would not want to lead off in the first paragraph with your main message: "You didn't get the job" or "You need to improve your interpersonal skills in dealing with customers." Thus you prepare the reader to hear your message by providing explanations first or cushioning the blow in some other way so that the reader will not be offended or "turned off" by your message.

The bad news pattern leads readers down a path, but in a way designed to let them down slowly to the disappointing news and then build up their confidence and goodwill again. Thus this particular approach is sometimes diagrammed like a "sandwich" to suggest the concepts of let-down followed by build-up.

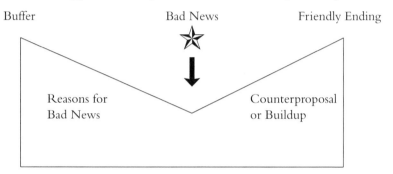

Although this pattern is usually best for disappointing messages, in some bad news situations you'll choose the direct approach of most important to least important order. For example, business people write warning or threatening letters only when a problem is serious, has lasted a long time, or the readers have failed or refused to deal with it. In these cases, it's important for the writer to make clear to the reader that the situation is serious and must be cleared up. While the tone will not be rude or unpleasant, the letter must be organized so that the reader doesn't miss the main point.

In both good news and bad news correspondences, the key to organizing them is knowing how to open. We'll look now at each strategy and how to construct the opening paragraph.

Exercise: Opening the Good or Neutral News Letter

Because delivering good or neutral news happens often in business, especially in letters and routine memoranda, it's important to become comfortable and skilled in executing this pattern of organization. You'll be using it every day.

An example of a typical neutral news letter is shown on the following page. It is a letter asking for action to solve a problem. Its clarity would be improved by a better opening paragraph that states its purpose up front.

Decide what the main point of this letter is. Why was it written? What action did the writer want from the reader? Record your answers to these questions in the spaces provided after the letter.

Good or Neutral News Letter Example

May 24, 1998

Mr. James A. Westing
Second Vice President
Jumbo Bank
Five New York Avenue
New York, NY 10018

Re: Acct. Nos. 1134565 & 7796009

Dear Mr. Westing:

It has been brought to my attention that for the past six months, we have not been receiving the bank statements for the subject accounts until the 18th of the following month. Last month, Jane Smitherson from our accounting department called to discuss this problem with John Davis, from Jumbo Bank's Statement Mailing Department. Mr. Davis informed us that the bank statements are mailed on the sixth day of each month. However, after that conversation, March's bank statements were not received until April 20th and April's bank statements were received on May 18th.

Due to our internal accounting and reconciliation deadlines, this creates a dilemma. We need to receive these statements no later than the 15th of each month.

This problem is hindering our ability to complete our accounting and reconciliation responsibilities in a timely manner. I am sure this is a minor issue which can be resolved.

Please feel free to call me at 212-523-0000 to discuss any further questions.

Your assistance in this matter is sincerely appreciated.

Sincerely yours,

Ann Knowles

1. Why was this letter written?

Your answer: _____

_____

2. What action did the writer want from the reader?

Your answer: _____

_____

Now write an opening paragraph for the letter that clearly states its purpose. Your goal is to state the main point of this letter right away. Include only as much background as needed to clarify the main message. You'll have plenty of time in the body of the letter to explain the reasons for what you want. Use the worksheet provided to write your opening paragraph.

Worksheet: Rewrite of Opening Paragraph of Good or Neutral News Letter

Sample Revision: Opening the Good or Neutral News Letter

Compare your opening to the samples below. These are only suggestions; yours will undoubtedly be a little different and may be better.

Example 1

We need to receive bank statements for the subject accounts by the 15th of each month to be able to meet our accounting and reconciliation deadlines. For the past six months, however, we have consistently received these statements three to five days late.

(In this example, the reference heading would be used as in the original letter.)

Example 2

For the past six months, we have consistently received bank statements for account numbers 1134565 and 7796009 three to five days late. To meet our accounting and reconciliation deadlines, we need to receive these statements in the future by the 15th of each month.

(In this example, the account numbers are included in the opening paragraph, making the reference heading unnecessary.)

Now look at a complete revision of the letter. Note that the body of the letter has been rewritten to dovetail with the opening paragraph. When the opening clearly states the main message, then the body is simply a matter of explaining that message more fully.

Sample Revision

May 24, 1998

Mr. James A. Westing

Second Vice President

Jumbo Bank

Five New York Avenue

New York, NY 10018

Dear Mr. Westing:

For the past six months, we have consistently received bank statements for account numbers 1134565 and 7796009 three to five days late. To meet our accounting and reconciliation deadlines, we need to receive these statements in the future by the 15th of each month.

Last month, Jane Smitherson of our accounting department discussed this problem with John Davis, a member of Jumbo Bank's Statement Mailing Department. Mr. Davis informed us that the bank statements are mailed on the sixth day of each month. However, after that conversation, the March bank statements were not received until April 20th. April's statements were received on May 18th.

We cannot complete our monthly responsibilities on time when these statements arrive three to five days late. I need your help to solve this problem.

Please call me at 212-523-0000 if you have any questions or need more information from me to help you clear this up.

Sincerely yours,

Ann Knowles

COMMENTARY: OPENING THE GOOD OR NEUTRAL NEWS LETTER

Do you notice any subtle tonal differences between this revision and the original letter? Which is stronger? Which is more likely to get the result the writer expects?

The original letter is written almost as though the writer thought it was a bad news letter. The key message is positioned in the middle, as our diagram of the bad news letter shows.

Notice, however, that this is not really a bad news letter. Its message is neutral. The reader will not be personally disappointed or upset that the bank is letting this customer down. This is a routine professional problem that requires solution. A true bad news message is one in which the reader's *personal* feelings are in jeopardy.

The writer of the original letter confused a routine business problem with a "bad news" situation. In using the bad news strategy to write her letter, she obscures the central request and, in fact, ultimately lets the reader off the hook: "I am sure this is a minor issue which can be resolved."

In the revised letter, the writer states immediately what she wants from the reader. She then directly enlists the reader's help after an explanation of her actions to date: "I need your help to solve this problem." The clarity and urgency of her request will more likely prompt the response she desires than the original version.

LANGUAGE AND TONE

Tone is a key element in successful business writing. I have defined it as how you say something or the "secondary message" you wish to communicate.

When you're speaking, of course, tone is really tone. It means the tonality or inflection you give words with your voice. A simple sentence such as "Okay, you're right," can be said in tones of agreement, incredulousness, frustration, or insult.

Letters and memos that have any aspect of bad news must be especially sensitive to the tone the language presents. Explanations must also be clearly and sensitively worded. Nothing is more annoying than receiving a disappointing message and being irritated by its tone at the same time.

In writing, you use a different set of tools to vary tone than you do in speaking. These tools are primarily descriptive words such as adjectives and adverbs, transition words and phrases, and the connotation and denotation of important words in the sentences. The kinds of explanations you give will also help establish your tone.

Consider the different tonal impact of these four sentences:

1. The company has a $300,000 debt.
2. The company has only a $300,000 debt.
3. The company owes a major debt of $300,000.
4. Although the company owes a $300,000 debt, it remains a good risk for more loans.

Describe the different impact of each statement. Notice words or phrases that define each sentence's message.

1. _____

2. _____

3. _____

4. _____

COMMENTARY: LANGUAGE AND TONE

1. The first sentence is a neutral statement of fact.
2. The second sentence minimizes the importance of the debt with the adverb *only*.
3. The third sentence describes the debt as serious by using the adjective *major*.

4. The fourth sentence minimizes the debt's importance in a subordinate clause, followed by a statement that interprets the debt's significance in a larger perspective.

These statements show how a writer's choice of language and information can change the same basic message.

EXERCISE: RESPONDING TO TONE

In a moment you'll read two letters about the same situation. Read these and decide which of the two you think would most effectively deliver its message and why.

On the worksheet following the letters, note your decision and some of the reasons for your decision.

Background

The two letters in this exercise are underwriting letters informing the reader that his health insurance policy has been terminated. The situation behind the letters is that the applicant was required to submit a blood test to be granted the policy. The recipient had paid the first insurance premium (more than $600) and had submitted the blood test. At the time this letter was written, however, the company had not received the test from the doctor. (This letter and the blood test literally crossed in the mail.)

Operating under its own internal deadlines for when the blood test should have been received (which, by the way, had not been told to the customer), the company terminated the policy and notified the customer by letter. Upon calling his agent, the customer found that the letter was primarily a warning to him about the importance of the blood test in the application process. His agent told him that the company was willing to process a second application with immediate temporary coverage, as long as the blood test requirement was met right away.

Given the situation, which was a real situation, you can imagine that the customer was unpleasantly surprised to receive this letter. The customer had not known about the submission deadline for the blood test until he received the letter and called his agent. The letter also informs him that, unbeknownst to him until this moment, he is walking around uninsured.

Put yourself in this customer's position. Which of the following two letters do you think would have been the least unpleasant to receive? Why?

Example 1

Dear Mr. Jones:

Thank you for considering SecurCo Company for your insurance needs.

I regret we are unable to offer the policy you requested at this time, because we have not received the results of your blood profile. If you are still interested in coverage, please contact your agent.

The enclosed underwriting notice provides details and procedures on your rights to access, disclosure and correction of information in our file.

If a payment was made with the application it is enclosed and any coverage under the temporary insurance agreement is ended.

We suggest you discuss any questions with your agent who is in a position to assist you.

Sincerely yours,

Jane Doe

Health Underwriting Department

*Refund to follow

Example 2

Dear Mr. Jones:

In reviewing your application for health insurance coverage, we find we have not received the results of your blood profile. Without this test, we are unable to offer the policy you requested.

If you have submitted your blood test, please contact your agent right away and tell him or her to notify me. However, your temporary insurance agreement is not in effect at this time and you will need to submit a new application for another insurance policy. If a payment was made with your original application, it will be forwarded to you in a few days.

The enclosed underwriting notice provides details and procedures on your rights to access, disclosure and correction of information in our file.

Thank you for considering SecurCo Company for your insurance needs. We will be glad to process another application for you that will provide you temporary coverage. Please contact your agent to assist you with another application.

Sincerely yours,

Jane Doe

Health Underwriting Department

Worksheet: Responding to Tone

I found Example _____ to have the most effective tone for the occasion and reader.

My reasons were:

COMMENTARY: RESPONDING TO TONE

Most people have found Example 2 to be more tonally effective for the reader and occasion. Here are some of the reasons they gave.

- Example 2 states the key message clearly in the first paragraph. The opening of Example 1 would confuse the reader. From his point of view, he did more than "consider" SecurCo: he sent the company a check for $600 and a blood sample.
- Example 2 explains what the reader must do to ensure that he has temporary coverage. It also gives him the "benefit of the doubt" that perhaps he did submit the blood sample: "If you have submitted you blood test, please contact your agent right away and tell him to notify me." Example 1 assumes that the test was not submitted and seems to offer the customer no way of rectifying his error, beyond the vague statement: "If you are still interested in coverage, please contact your agent."
- Example 2 offers to process another application to ensure temporary coverage. Example 1 washes its hands of the customer: "We suggest you discuss any questions with your agent who is in a position to assist you."
- Example 2 says the customer will get a refund in a few days. Example 1 says the refund is enclosed, then scribbles a hasty footnote at the bottom: "Refund to follow."

STATING BAD NEWS TACTFULLY

Sometimes you must refuse or disappoint someone in the business world. Some typical situations are

- Denying a request
- Stating a negative decision
- Turning down a person's application for a job

Professionals seek to maintain the goodwill of customers and associates as much as possible. It is precisely when you must disappoint someone that maintaining goodwill is most difficult.

Delivering bad news requires an understanding of human psychology. You know that when you refuse people something they consider their due, they will be disappointed and frustrated unless you give justifying reasons. Given human nature, however, if you begin with the refusal, the person will be disappointed at the least and may even be angered. An angry person is not a logical person. Thus even if your reasons for the refusal are good, they may fall on deaf ears as the person smarts over the refusal. In the case of a letter written this way, he or she may even stop reading after the first paragraph and throw the letter away. In such cases, the reasons for the refusal are never heard.

However, if you start the letter off pleasantly and give justifying reasons before stating the refusal, your reader is more likely to accept the bad news because you have shown the logic behind it. This is commonsensical psychology that we use in our dealings with people every day.

Thus organization of a bad news letter can be described simply. You begin by cushioning the blow of the refusal by trying to open with a fact (pleasant, if possible) about the situation on which both the reader and writer can agree. This is commonly called a "buffer." In it, you set the stage for a review of the facts of the case. You also try to establish, through your tone, that you are a reasonable and friendly person.

After you establish compatibility in the opening paragraph, if you can, give the reasons that you cannot do what the reader wants or expects. (In some cases, such as turning down a person's job application, you cannot always reveal the reasons—perhaps the selection was made by committee and someone on the committee disliked the applicant, some other applicant had an "inside track," etc.) These reasons should be stated carefully and factually.

After presenting your case thoroughly and tactfully, you reveal the bad news. **It should be minimally but clearly stated.** Finally, you should, if possible, end on a note of favorable interest to your reader that demonstrates your and your company's goodwill. In some situations you may be able to offer the reader something else in lieu of what he or she wanted; this is called a counterproposal.

Exercise: Tonal Components of Bad News Letters

To get a sense of this form in action, let's look now at the "classic" letter of this type: the letter refusing a job application.

After you've read the two examples, list the components of tone that you found were successful or unsuccessful in each. Write your observations on the worksheet provided.

Example 1 Bad News Letter

Dear Mr. Jones:

The selection committee has carefully reviewed the material submitted by all the applicants for the position of Accounting Director of the Finance Division at SYZ Insurance Company. Three outstanding finalists have been selected for this position. This letter is to inform you that you will not be considered for this position.

It is unfortunate that we have only one position to fill, for we had 100 highly qualified people apply for this job. The large number of qualified applicants made the selection of finalists especially difficult.

We appreciate your interest in SYZ Insurance Company and extend our best wishes for your continued success.

Sincerely,

Charlene Walters

Example 2 Bad News Letter

Dear Mr. Smith:

Thank you for participating in the final interviews with members of our Board of Directors for the position of Executive Director of the Philadelphia branch of American Insurers Association. We appreciated your candid and clear responses to our many inquiries.

I regret to inform you that we have chosen another applicant for the position. It is unfortunate that I have only one position to fill at the Association at this time. Your presentation to the members of the Board showed me that you would be a most valued colleague in our work. Should the occasion arise when I may need to call on you for some special projects for the Association, I would hope that you would be available.

We are part of an intricate network in the insurance community because our programs are so broadly based in Philadelphia and the surrounding areas. If you would agree, I would like to pass your resume and materials to people I think would benefit from your expertise and in whose programs you would be an asset.

I wish you all the best and success in your career.

Sincerely,

Harriett Plains

Worksheet: Tonal Components of Bad News Letters

Example 1

Tonal Successes	Tonal Failures

Example 2

Tonal Successes	Tonal Failures

COMMENTARY: TONAL COMPONENTS OF BAD NEWS LETTERS

Example 1

Tonal Successes	Tonal Failures
Ends on a friendly note.	Sets the reader up for a positive message and then lets him down (see first paragraph).
	Does not make clear whether the reader was one of the "100 highly qualified applicants."

The first letter could have been retrieved simply by thanking the reader for the application and giving the reasons for the refusal before the bad news. Given the opening paragraph, however, many readers would not read on to hear the reasonableness and politeness of the second and third paragraphs. Such letters can leave a lasting negative impression of the company represented by the letter.

Example 2

Tonal Successes	Tonal Failures
Thanks the reader for his application (neutral opening). States the refusal clearly, but minimally. States the refusal clearly, but minimally.	Does not explain why the reader did not get the job. (Note that in rejection letters, writers may be unable to explain the reasons for rejection. What if the applicant was not hired because some-

Encourages the reader by assuring him that he was qualified for the job, even though he did not get it.

Offers a concrete counterproposal.

one else had an inside track or one person on the selection committee didn't like the applicant? Clearly, these kinds of reasons could not be put on paper.)

The second letter, although unable to explain the reasons why the person did not get the job, is exceedingly diplomatic and personal. The writer gives the clear impression that he thought highly of the candidate. In addition, the counterproposal of sending the candidate's resume to other organizations would undoubtedly ease the disappointment of the refusal.

Exercise: Revising a Bad News Letter

The examples you just saw are fairly dramatic. It's easy to see how a writer when refusing a person's job application should take care to show sensitivity to the reader's feelings. It's more difficult to take the time to use the bad news strategy in routine refusal situations where it's standard practice to handle the recipient of the letter in a somewhat heavy-handed way.

The letter that follows is a standard letter refusing a customer's claim for disability benefits. Using the worksheet provided, revise this letter into bad news form. Make the tone more personal and tactful.

Sample Letter

Dear Mr. James:

After thoroughly reviewing your claim for Short-Term Disability (STD) benefits, we regret to advise you that at this time we cannot approve your claim for the period of 10/28/97 through 11/6/97.

Unfortunately, based on the information received, we are unable to approve your claim due to insufficient medical substantiation of total disability beginning on 10/28/97. Your doctor did not indicate the health reasons or diagnosis involved in causing you to stop work on the above date.

In order for your claim for STD benefits to be reconsidered, you must submit the required medical verification on your Statement of Claim form. To do this, please complete Section A and have your doctor complete Section B of the enclosed claim form. The completed form should be returned directly to my attention in the enclosed self-addressed envelope.

If we do not hear from you within 10 working days, your office will be advised to process a Personal Leave of Absence without salary for the period of 10/28/97 through 11/6/97.

Your prompt attention to this matter would be appreciated and if you have any questions, please call me at 212-523-8888.

Worksheet: Revising a Bad News Letter

SAMPLE REVISION: BAD NEWS LETTER

Use this revision as a benchmark to evaluate your own work. Notice in the sample revision how the writer uses all of the elements of the bad news strategy: buffer, reasons, minimally stated bad news message, counterproposal, and friendly ending.

Dear Mr. James:

We have reviewed your claim for Short-Term Disability (STD) benefits.

To date, we have received insufficient medical substantiation that your total disability began on 10/28/97. Your doctor did not indicate on the claim form what the diagnosis or health reasons were that caused you to stop work on that date. We are therefore unable to approve your claim.

We will have to advise your office to process a Personal Leave of Absence without salary for the period of 10/28/97 through 11/6/97 unless you submit the required medical verification within 10 working days. To help you resubmit your claim quickly, I have enclosed another claim form. Please complete Section A yourself and then have your doctor complete Section B. Return the form directly to me in the enclosed self-addressed envelope.

If you have any questions, please call me at 212-523-8888.

CHAPTER 9

Using Formatting Techniques

Catching the Reader's Eye
Types of Formatting Techniques
Becoming Sensitive to Format

CATCHING THE READER'S EYE

If you want your readers to follow you along a path of logic, you must act as their guide along the way. Your three major techniques for keeping them on the path are readability, organization, and formatting.

Readability is a writer's major technique for establishing and sustaining the reader's interest. The organization a writer chooses must follow the pattern that makes sense for presenting the document's content. Format is the way the writer lays out the written material visually.

Many writers may think of layout as a less important area of writing than logic and prose style, in the same way that painting and sculpture are viewed by some as higher art forms than graphic design. However, because we live in a world that has become very sensitive to visual stimuli, business readers, like other modern readers, seem to find format an especially useful aid to readability.

In short, format complements organization to help readers follow the report by *eye* as well as by logic. The various formatting techniques are visual methods of highlighting or emphasizing important points or sections of a document. They can also serve an organizing, classifying, or labeling function. A format can greatly help or hinder readability.

Formatting is one of the most creative and personal aspects of editing. The techniques that exist may be applied in a number of ways. It's also possible to create a new technique in certain situations. But the final test of a good format is that it helps the reader see logical relationships, emphasizes important points, and in general contributes to the economy and coherence of the writing.

The problem many writers have with format is that they become too attached to one or two techniques rather than thinking about what techniques might genuinely improve the organization and readability of a particular piece of writing. For example, many writers in business today have become enamored of the "bullet point." I once spoke to a vice president of a major corporation who believed that all reports could be constructed entirely in bullet points, and actually instructed his subordinates to write all memoranda in bullet points. He hoped this directive would decrease the amount of bad writing he had to read every day.

This is an example of missing the point (pun intended) where formatting techniques are concerned. Formatting techniques are not and never will be a substitute for a clear, readable prose style—as this vice president soon found out. The reports he received in bullets points were even more unreadable than the reports he had received in prose.

Because formatting is part of editing, it is generally the last thing you do after you make your prose style readable. Once you've established the logic your ideas should follow and have attempted a first draft, you then see whether techniques such as subheadings or lists could in some way improve the report's organization and ease of reading.

Sometimes a company suggests or requires a format or template. Here the danger is to see the format as a formula for writing in which you simply "fill in the blanks." Generally, a suggested format is only the barest skeletal outline of the logic a document should take, along with some suggestions concerning the data to be included. In any given structure, many formats within the sections are possible, but you are still faced with the task of achieving coherence from section to section.

Let's take time now to learn about the different kinds of formatting techniques business writers use.

TYPES OF FORMATTING TECHNIQUES

The major types of formatting techniques used in business writing are

- Instructive and topical subheadings
- Bullet points or lists
- Indenting, underlining, and capitalizing

- White space
- Appendices
- T-forms or parallel columns

INSTRUCTIVE AND TOPICAL SUBHEADINGS

Subheadings are a good way to make large prose sections of reports and memoranda more accessible to readers. The writer divides the material into small, digestible units, and the subheading itself is used to label the content of the units.

There are two types of subheadings: instructive and topical.

Topical subheadings identify topics that will be discussed in a section: for example, Company Profile, Credit and Marketing, Recommendations. They are the most general type of subheadings.

Instructive subheadings are more specific than topical subheadings. They identify a theme or state a point that a section will develop. Company Risks Shrinking Market Share or Payment Schedule Not Met are instructive subheadings.

BULLET POINTS OR LISTS

Bullet points are a formatting technique in which a printer's dot (•) is placed next to an item, sentence, or paragraph instead of a number. Lists are composed of a series of these bulleted or numbered items, sentences, or paragraphs.

Avoid writing sentences that contain lists unless the lists are very short. Generally, *three* items in a series is all a single sentence can handle, and these items should not be long, complex phrases.

When vertical lists are used, items should be phrased similarly. Don't mix sentences, phrases, and simple nouns. In grammatical terminology, this is the principle of *parallelism* or parallel construction. Parallelism means using corresponding syntactical forms for all items.

Good example	*Bad example*
1. Sell excess inventory	1. Company should sell excess inventory
2. Reduce level of A/R's	2. A/R's—reduce
3. Limit bank's exposure	3. Limiting bank's exposure

INDENTING, UNDERLINING, AND CAPITALIZING

These techniques basically help you catch the reader's eye in order to emphasize points in your document. They should not be overused. For example, if you underline a number of words in a section to achieve emphasis, the eye will become confused and you will achieve exactly the opposite of your objective.

WHITE SPACE

This is another visual technique to help readers assimilate the written page. It also has a psychological dimension. Most people's hearts sink when they see a page black with type. It looks formidable even if it isn't. Reading a written page without margins, where each line runs to the very edge of the page—so much so that the ends of words literally run off the line—is also an irritating experience. You must *motivate* your readers to find your work accessible and attractive.

APPENDICES

Webster's defines an appendix as "supplementary matter added at the end of a book." Unlike books, most reports and certainly most memoranda would not be broad enough in scope to warrant appendices. In theory, memoranda are limited in scope and self-contained.

Occasionally, however, the subject of a report or memorandum warrants extensive research. When writing the explanation section, you may find that even though you do not need to include certain information in the document's body, it would be helpful to supply that information to the reader in an appendix.

When faced with this situation, the writer must be careful to cross-reference the information at the exact point in the text where the material would ordinarily have been presented. A cross-reference is generally noted in parentheses at the point where readers would logically have read the material: for example, "(See Appendix I)."

An appendix may be referenced in the text in several ways. If there are several appendices, the cross-references can read "See Appendix I," or "See Appendix II." The appendices themselves, when they appear at the end of the report, should also each be given an instructive title, such as "Five Changing Demographic Trends of the 90s." An instructive title directs the reader to the appendix's topic. If the report contains only one appendix, you can cross-reference by title: See appendix entitled "Five Changing Demographic Trends of the 90s."

A word of warning: Don't use an appendix as a "dumping ground" for research you've done that readers do not really need to know. They will not be impressed, nor will they read it, unless it clearly amplifies their knowledge in a relevant way.

T-Forms or Parallel Columns

"T-Forms" are a fairly new entrant in the formatting field, whereas parallel columns have always been around. The techniques are basically the same: *comparing* or *contrasting* lists of information or points.

The difference is a minor point of layout. You can present your contrasting lists under a T-form or simply line the lists up next to each other using bullet points or numbers. In either case, you'll usually label each column, using either a phrase or a statement that clarifies the purpose of the comparison.

T-Form

Business memoranda are generally characterized by . . .	Essays are generally characterized by . . .
•	•
•	•

Parallel columns

Business memoranda are generally characterized by . . .	Essays are generally characterized by . . .
•	•
•	•

BECOMING SENSITIVE TO FORMAT

Choosing from this smorgasbord of possible formatting techniques involves creativity and personal preference. There may be a number of techniques that could work well in improving readability. Thus you'll need to become familiar with the choices and how to use them.

To increase your sensitivity to formatting techniques, on the next two pages you'll see presented an unformatted example followed by a formatted example. Be aware of the kinds of techniques used to reformat the example so that the reader can identify the points and follow the logic more easily.

Example 1

You've already learned to state your basic position to your reader in a lead paragraph. Once you've gotten your main points down, you need to decide how to explain them. Clearly, you've only caught the skeleton of your case in the lead. The rest of the memorandum must "flesh out" that skeleton.

You'll recall we spoke earlier about a couple of thought processes to use to organize paragraphs. Let me refresh your memory. Cause and effect analysis means explaining why an event had a certain result or how a certain result stemmed from a particular event. Comparison and contrast means comparing a group of similarities, a group of differences, or a combination of the two in explaining a general point. Now I'll add a definition of a third process. Giving examples is the way we illustrate a general point with concrete details.

Example 1 (Revised)

Explaining Your Lead

You've already learned to state your basic position to your reader in a lead paragraph.

Once you've gotten your main points down, you need to decide how to explain them. Clearly, you've only caught the skeleton of your case in the lead. The rest of the memorandum must "flesh out" that skeleton.

You'll recall we spoke earlier about a couple of thought processes as ways of organizing paragraphs. Let me refresh your memory:

> *Cause and effect analysis* means explaining why an event had a certain result or how a certain result stemmed from a particular event.

> *Comparison and contrast* means comparing a group of similarities, a group of differences, or a combination of the two in explaining a general point.

Now I'll add a definition of a third process:

> *Giving examples* is the way we *illustrate* a general point with concrete details.

EXAMPLE 2

Business memoranda are generally characterized by direct, to-the-point organization. This means that conclusions, a thesis, or recommendations are stated first, followed by supporting arguments or explanation. The memo closes with requests for action or follow-up that the writer wants from the reader.

Essays, on the other hand, are characterized by more leisurely, exploratory organization. Generally, the writer introduces his or her thesis or main point to whet the reader's appetite. He or she then explores and explains that point and related points in the body of the essay. The piece usually ends in a concluding section in which the writer restates the main point in a more trenchant way.

Memo writers generally do not feel as much freedom to explore subordinate points as do essay writers. Thus the explanation of main points in a memo is usually highly selective and closely related to the main points stated at the beginning of the memo. Essayists have more leeway to explore interesting subordinate issues that, while related to the thesis, may not be of central importance to the arguments supporting the thesis.

EXAMPLE 2 (REVISED)

Business memoranda are generally characterized by . . .	Essays are generally characterized by . . .
• Direct, to-the-point organization	• More leisurely organization
• Conclusions or recommendations stated first, followed by explanation and arguments	• Main point stated first to whet the reader's appetite, followed by explanation of the main point in the body of the essay
• Closing request for any follow-up the writer wants from the reader	• Concluding section in which the writer restates the main point in a more trenchant way

Exercise: Working with Formatting Techniques

Example 1 used three techniques to format the text: shorter paragraphs, white space, and underlining.

Example 2 made use of parallel columns to reformat the prose text. This kind of format usually requires the writer to recast the text to achieve readability between the columns. Although parallel columns do not have to be as strictly parallel as lists, writers should try to use approximately the same kind of phrasing and syntactical forms between corresponding points.

Below is a prose example and a list of several formatting techniques to improve its readability. Choose *at least two* techniques that you think would work well together to reformat the example. On the worksheet provided, lay out the example using your chosen techniques. You need not fill in every word of the text unless you want to. If you use subheadings, however, you should write them out.

Prose Example

The first thing readers will read in your memorandum is the briefing. Therefore, it's important for you to be able to start them off on the right foot rather than confusing them or putting them off in some way.

In short, good briefings can be distinguished from bad briefings in several outstanding ways.

A good briefing presents only background information that is absolutely necessary for readers to have. Additionally, it sets the stage for the kind of writing style readers can expect and begins the process of motivating them to read the entire memorandum. If one part of the memo must be exquisitely well written, it is the briefing. Edit and rewrite until the prose is a polished gem.

A bad briefing generally starts by putting readers off in one or more ways. Sometimes the writer presents a lot of facts that, while interesting, do not really prepare readers for the case that will ultimately be presented. Sometimes a writer will immediately adopt an inappropriate tone—for example, taking a challenging or confrontational position with a reader the writer knows is hostile. In such instances, it's better to work the case up more slowly. Even worse is the tendency of some writers to start readers off with a turgidly written lump of ill-digested or poorly organized facts and statistics. The readers' first impulse, in such cases, is usually to trash the memo. Remember, first impressions count in writing too.

Check off at least two techniques you think you could use together to revise this passage.

_____ white space

_____ instructive subheadings

_____ topical subheadings

_____ underlining

_____ capitalizing

_____ parallel columns

_____ bullet points

Now lay out the example using the techniques you've chosen.

Worksheet: Working with Formatting Techniques

SUGGESTED REVISION:
WORKING WITH FORMATTING TECHNIQUES

You could probably choose any two formatting techniques and, if they are properly applied, the result would improve the readability of the passage.

In a moment I'll show you two sample revisions. In Revision 1, the formatting techniques used were boldface, bullet points, and parallel columns.

Revision 2 uses instructive subheadings, white space, boldface, italics, and bullet points to format the text. The paragraphs have been shortened and the topic sentences made clearer (see the first sentence of each paragraph).

Although I did not ask you to rewrite the paragraphs, always remember that style and organization are still your two most important tools for achieving readability.

As you read these examples and look at your own work, keep in mind that format is one of the most personal and creative aspects of writing. As long as the format makes reading the text easier rather than harder, it is probably effective. Format, however, cannot be used as a substitute for writing.

See if your layout is similar to, or perhaps even better than, these two examples.

REVISION 1

The briefing should . . .	Be careful the briefing doesn't . . .
• Present only necessary background information.	• Present a lot of facts that may be interesting but do not really prepare the reader for the case stated in the memo.
• Help readers feel receptive to the idea of reading the memo. Tone is an important technique for enticing and motivating readers to want to read your work.	• Put readers off in some way—for example, immediately adopting a challenging or confrontational position with readers you know are hostile. Work your case up more slowly.
• Set the stage for the memo's writing style. If one part of the memo must be exquisitely well-written, it is the briefing. Edit! Rewrite! And edit again! Make it a polished gem.	• Start readers off with a turgidly written lump of ill-digested and poorly organized facts and statistics. Their first impulse will be to trash the memo. Remember, first impressions count in writing too.

REVISION 2

First Impressions Count

The first thing readers will read in your memorandum is the briefing. It's important for you to be able to start them off on the right foot. You want to avoid:

- confusing them, or
- putting them off in some way.

Confusing the Readers

Confusing the readers usually results when you present a lot of irrelevant facts at the beginning of the memorandum. If the briefing does not really prepare readers for the case that will ultimately be presented, it will confuse them. Even worse is the tendency of some writers to start readers off with a turgidly written lump of ill-digested or poorly organized facts and statistics. In such cases, both form and content are confusing and the readers' first impulse will usually be to trash the memo.

Putting the Readers Off

The writing style of the briefing will either motivate readers to keep reading or make them want to stop reading. If one part of a memorandum must be exquisitely well-written, it is the briefing. *Edit* and *rewrite* until the prose is a polished gem.

Another way writers can put their readers off right away is by the tone they adopt. An example is taking a challenging or confrontational position with a reader you know is hostile to your case. In such instances, it's better to work your case up more slowly.

CHAPTER 10

Using Graphics

Designing Graphics
Helping the Reader Assimilate a Graphic

DESIGNING GRAPHICS

Charts, tables, and graphs are used to illustrate comparisons of data or variables. A writer should choose to use them when, to repeat an old saw, a picture is worth a thousand words. The problem for most writers is that they often do not recognize when a tabular or graphic presentation would be much clearer and simpler than an explanation in prose. Here's an example of what I mean:

> The results of the technical and economic evaluations are listed in the order of increasing annual cost in the attached summary sheets. Rego Computing and J&E Computers are lowest in cost. Rego Computing and Allied Electric are technically rated one and two, respectively. Allied Electric is about two times the cost of the two low vendors. An award based solely on the results of the invitation would recommend Rego Computing. However, a partial award to J&E Computers is also recommended to provide a backup system, at negligible difference in cost, in the event Rego Computer is unable to meet our schedule requirements. In addition, it is recommended that Allied Electric be awarded an annual order for programs currently being run at Allied Electric facilities. The recommended authorization for Allied Electric provides funds to phase out Allied Electric usage over a 6-month period, which period is required to minimize loss of productivity and personnel retraining problems.

Now turn the page and look at a table the writer was able to come up with to organize these comparisons more simply.

Vendor	Cost	Technical Rating	Recommendations
Rego Computer	Lowest	First	_____
			_____
			_____
			_____
J&E Computers	Same as Rego	Third or ??	_____
			_____
			_____
			_____
Allied Electric	Two times Rego & J&E Computers	Second	_____
			_____
			_____
			_____

In this example, some prose would still be necessary to help the reader make sense of the table. The recommendations would be written in prose and perhaps a brief cover memorandum or summary paragraph would introduce the purpose of the table. Finally, the table should have a title that pinpoints its message.

In short, you should use a table, chart, or graph to explain relationships that do not easily lend themselves to prose explanation. Selecting what form of graphic to use, once you've identified the need for a visual presentation, will depend on your content.

Tables are used to organize information in a matrix or grid. The reader is usually invited to read both vertically and horizontally. Tables only imply relationships and are the least visual kind of graphic. They help your reader know how you've classified information.

Charts and graphs, on the other hand, *demonstrate* relationships visually. They should be used to reinforce messages that are not clear from tabular data alone.

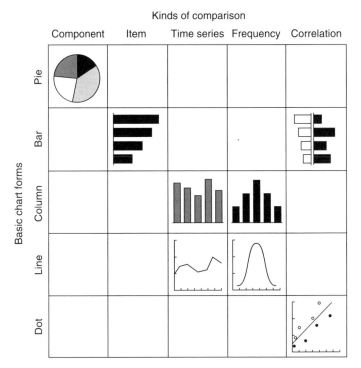

Figure 1

Most charts are variations on the same forms: pie, bar, column, curve (sometimes called surface charts), and dot (sometimes called line charts). Each form illustrates certain kinds of relationships better than others.

Look at a matrix[1] that matches five standard types of comparisons (shown across the top) with the five basic chart forms (listed down the side) (Fig. 1).

This matrix is an excellent illustration of the power of graphics. Think how many words it would take me to explain its content.

The problem report writers most often encounter when they decide to illustrate a point graphically is *identifying their message*. I've already noted that sometimes a futile attempt to explain a series of comparisons in prose may lead you to the revelation that a graphic can make the point more simply and clearly. However, the most straightforward way to design a graphic is first to identify your message and then think about the appropriate graphic format.

[1]Gene Zelazny, *Say It with Charts: The Executive's Guide to Successful Presentations* (Homewood, IL: Dow Jones-Irwin, 1985), p. 27. Reproduced with permission of The McGraw-Hill Companies.

Any number of messages might be illustrated by a given set of data. Consider these data:

Percentage of MBAs Hired This Year by Region

	Co. X	Co. Y
North	25%	35%
South	25%	30%
East	10%	20%
West	40%	15%

If the message you want to illustrate is simply a percentage breakdown of new hires by region, then this table is the appropriate format and the title correctly identifies its message.

However, suppose your message was that the companies favor hiring MBAs from different regions. Then you'd need a different format to demonstrate this message clearly (Fig. 2).

Now suppose your message was that Company X hires its largest percentage of MBAs from the West, where Company Y hires its smallest percentage of MBAs (Fig. 3).

The form your graphic will take depends entirely on your message. Without that message clearly in mind, you're flying blind. Or as one authority puts it: "Choosing

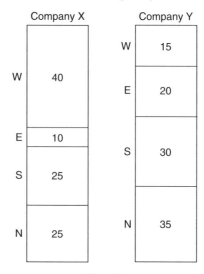

Figure 2

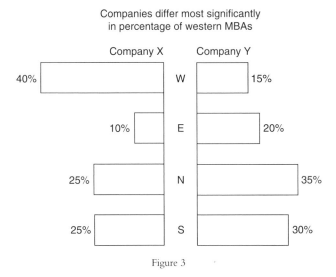

Figure 3

a chart form without a message in mind is like trying to color coordinate your wardrobe while blindfolded."[2]

Sometimes report writers needlessly make problems for themselves with graphics. They know readers like them so they try to use them. In doing so, they sometimes miss the most fundamental point about graphics: readers like them *when they make a point clear.* Just like poorly written prose, a graphic without a clear message slows the reader down and impedes the writing's readability.

HELPING THE READER ASSIMILATE A GRAPHIC

Once you've designed a graphic, you help your readers assimilate its message by

- Stating the message in a title; and
- Placing the graphic where the reader needs to see it.

In titling graphics, avoid general-topic titles and instead pinpoint the message you want readers to see in the graphic. Good titles *instruct* the reader to look at something specific. Consider the same chart with different titles (Fig. 4).

The second chart will be easier for readers to comprehend because its title states its message more precisely. Chart titles must do more than state the topic: they must direct the reader's eyes to see something in the chart.

[2]Zelazny, p. 11.

Figure 4

Because a general title will not direct readers to the comparison you wish to highlight, they may focus on a comparison you did not intend (Fig. 5).

Given such a general title, a reader might focus upon one of several messages implied in the data:

- The number of new employees has decreased.

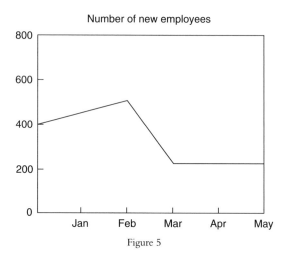

Figure 5

- The highest number of new employees was hired in February.
- The number of new employees dipped sharply in March.
- The same number of employees was hired in April and May.

You must tell readers which of these messages you consider most important for them to see.

Once you pinpoint your message, the title itself states that message clearly and concisely, the way newspaper headlines do. Here are some topic titles that have been turned into instructive titles:

Topic title:	Percentage of Sales by Division
Instructive title:	Widget Division Accounts for 54% of Sales
Topic title:	Construction Demographic Trends
Instructive title:	New Construction Grows in the Southwest
Topic title:	Relationship of Owners' Salaries and Profits
Instructive title:	Owners' Salaries Are Weakening Company Profits

When writing titles, keep the tone factual. Avoid headlines that suggest the tabloid style: "New Construction Skyrockets in the Southwest."

Once you've designed your graphic and titled it, show it *at the exact moment* that you want readers to see it. In general, this means integrating the graphic into the report text.

The reason for this generalization is that a graphic loses some of its immediate illustrative power when readers must go searching for it. This applies to all sorts of graphics: pictures, diagrams, charts, flowcharts, graphs, or tables. Thus appendices are best used for supplemental information.

An exceptional situation might occur when you have many graphics to show and including them all in the text might fragment the report. In such cases, you would show the graphics as appendices and cross-refer readers at the exact moment you want them to look at a particular graphic. In addition to titling each graphic in the appendices, you need to label them in order: Appendix 1, Appendix 2, etc. Your cross-reference can refer to the shorter label rather than the longer title: for example, "See Appendix 1."

In longer research reports, the report is often printed and bound like a book. In such cases, graphics are usually given a page or part of a page next to the prose text in the same way that pictures and illustrations are displayed in a hard-bound book. Readers are then cross-refered to the page or place where they can find a particular graphic when they read the section of the text that explains its purpose.

Whether a graphic is integrated into the text or relegated to an appendix, *its point should be stated in the text* as well as in its title. This is most often accomplished by commenting on the graphic with a prose statement of its point, showing the graphic, and then perhaps commenting further on its implications. Or you might provide a general introduction to the graphic in the text, show it, and then state its main point and comment on it.★ You've seen me use both these approaches a number of times in this lesson. Let me recall one example to refresh your memory:

> In titling graphics, avoid general-topic titles and instead pinpoint the message you want readers to see in the graphic. Good titles instruct the reader to look at something specific. Consider the same chart with different titles (Fig. 6).
>
> The second chart will be easier for readers to comprehend because its title states its message more precisely. Chart titles must do more than state the topic: they must direct the reader's eyes to see something in the chart.

This time, I've underlined the point in the text that the graphic illustrates.

Always remember that stating a graphic's purpose clearly in the text and explaining its implications in readable prose remain your most powerful tools for helping readers assimilate it. Graphics should *never* be used as a substitute for stating a point and explaining it clearly in prose. The text is the most important part of a document and will always occupy the center stage.

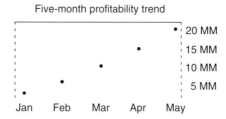

Figure 6

★Sometimes when a graphic is integrated into the text, the title will be redundant and may be omitted.

Exercise, Part 1: Designing a Graphic Format

Perhaps the most important skill you'll need in designing graphics is the ability to recognize when a table, chart, or graph would help present your content better than prose alone. Then you need to be able to design an appropriate graphic format that conveys a message simply and, you hope, memorably.

Read the paragraph shown in the example. I think you'll agree that one reason it's hard to read is that it attempts to explain a series of comparisons in prose. Your task is to present this message more simply and clearly. To do this, you'll need to

- Pinpoint the part of the message you want to show in a graphic
- Choose a form for the graphic
- State the message of the graphic in an instructive title
- Combine the graphic with a prose commentary on its message

Example

The cost of the current JV Computer Training Tutorial is $50,000 a year. The Lark Tutorial is superior and we should consider installing it, even though initial installation would cost $60,000. The current JV Tutorial will continue to cost $50,000 each year, whereas the second-year cost of the Lark Tutorial would only be $5,000 and $3,000 for each year thereafter. By installing the Lark Tutorial, we could save about $45,000 in the second year and about $47,000 for each year after that.

Your Presentation

Exercise, Part 2: Designing a Graphic Format

Three possible graphic presentations of the paragraph are shown on the next two pages. Compare your presentation with these. Then decide which one you think is the most effective, next effective, down to least effective. Be sure to include yours in the ranking; it may be better than any of these.

After you've judged all of the examples, record your ranking in the spaces provided. Also record a couple of reasons for your decisions.

Your Ranking

Most effective _____   Why? _____

Next effective _____   Why? _____

Next effective _____   Why? _____

Least effective _____   Why? _____

Example 1

We should install the Lark Computer Training Tutorial because it's superior to ours and will be cheaper in the long run.

Comparative Costs

	This Year	Next Year	Thereafter
JV	$50,000	$50,000	$50,000
Lark	$60,000	$5,000	$3,000

Although we'll spend $10,000 more for Lark the first year, the ultimate savings after that will be enormous: $45,000 the second year and $47,000 per year for each subsequent year.

Example 2

I recommend installing the Lark Computer Training Tutorial in place of our JV Tutorial. As the accompanying graph shows (Fig. 7), the initial cost of installation will

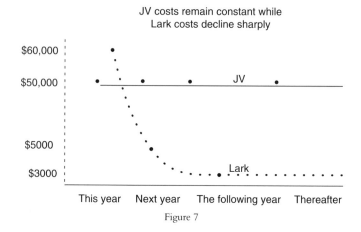

Figure 7

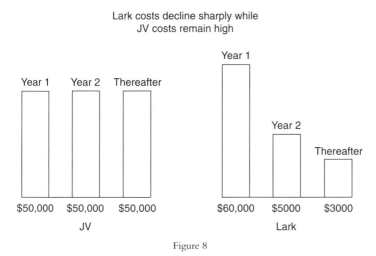

Figure 8

be higher than the price we now pay for JV, but the savings in subsequent years will be substantial.

Example 3

We should install the Lark Computer Training Tutorial in place of the JV Tutorial we now use. The columns in the chart (Fig. 8) show that, after an initially higher cost of installation, Lark will be considerably cheaper in subsequent years than JV.

COMMENTARY: DESIGNING A GRAPHIC FORMAT

Once again, I cannot provide commentary on your example, but I am providing commentary on the three examples shown. Use my comments to help you evaluate your example and your ranking of all the examples.

Example 1

This is probably the simplest and perhaps the clearest way to revise the example. The table clears up the major readability problem in the paragraph.

In addition to using a table to organize the cost comparisons, the writer introduces the table with a statement that directs the reader's attention to the salient point illustrated in the table—"cheaper in the long run." She also discusses some implications of the table afterwards. The table's general-topic title, however, does not pinpoint its message and should be revised.

Example 2

The primary visual value of the line graph is the picture it presents of the decline in Lark's costs after one year. The instructive title reinforces this message. The prose commentary, however, mentions an aspect of the data that is not emphasized in the chart: *savings*. The writer might also discuss the savings that result from the lost declines.

Example 3

Some might argue that the data being presented are too simple for a graphic presentation of this sort. But the bar charts illustrate the comparison more dramatically and perhaps more memorably than the other two charts. The prose commentary and the instructive title also dovetail nicely to direct the eye to the graphic's message.

When choosing a graphic presentation, you may find there are several that could work. You'll usually choose the one that's the simplest—in this case, the table is the simplest presentation. If, however, you're especially concerned about impact, you may select "drama" as one of your criteria in designing a graphic.

FINAL THOUGHTS

Dear Reader:

Congratulations! You have now completed the equivalent of what you'd receive in most college-level or executive-level courses in business writing.

I had two major goals in writing this book. The first was to encourage you to write in your own voice rather than in a style that imitates someone else's voice. If you've learned nothing else from this book, I hope you've learned that it's okay to speak out and be yourself when you write.

I realize this is easier said than done. We've discussed why people fear being open and honest in their writing. And our great English literary tradition, which I've made reference to throughout this book, is both a burden and a gift. Many believe there's some sort of "absolute standard of good writing" floating out there in space, like a platonic ideal, that they have little hope of measuring up to.

As I've mentioned before, though, what you really should do is develop your own standards and measure up to those. To do this, you should learn from the accomplishments of other writers rather than merely imitate them. Trust the education you've received, trust your instincts, continue to read critically, and make conscious choices about how you will write. This is the only way you will ever feel confident about your work or develop any real facility.

My second goal was, I think, more important. We live in an age when perhaps the most fundamental principle of good writing and, indeed, of all human communication has been forgotten. Communication happens when one human being connects, either positively or negatively, with another human being. Computers may deliver information more quickly, but they are only the transmitter, not the communicator. And while all of us who work in business must admit that corporate politics exist, we must still attempt to keep the independent voice alive—the voice that possesses the courage to speak its convictions clearly and honestly.

If you're going to write for the purpose of communicating, you'll have to come out into the open. And you'll need solid tools and techniques to start carving out your message.

I hope you've acquired some techniques and gained some confidence. Good luck with your writing.

Sincerely yours,

Olivia Stockard

Olivia Stockard

SOURCES CITED

Burroughs, Edgar Rice. *Tarzan of the Apes.* New York: Ballantine Books, January 1976.

Lanham, Richard A. *Revising Prose.* New York: Charles Scribner's Sons, 1979.

McCrum, Robert; Cran, William; and MacNeil, Robert. *The Story of English.* New York: Elisabeth Sifton Books, Viking, 1986.

Orwell, George. "Politics and the English Language." Reprinted in *A Collection of Essays by George Orwell.* New York: Harcourt, Brace, Jovanovich, Harbrace Paperbound Library, 1953.

Strunck, William, Jr. *The Elements of Style, With Revisions, an Introduction, and a Chapter on Writing by E.B. White.* Third Edition. Needham Heights, MA: Allyn & Bacon, 1979.

Skyrms, Brian. *Choice and Chance: An Introduction to Inductive Logic.* Third Edition. Belmont, CA: Wadsworth, 1986.

The New York Times. "Obituary of Dr. Rudolf Flesch," October 7, 1986.

Zelazny, Gene. *Say It with Charts: The Executive's Guide to Successful Presentations.* Homewood, IL: Dow Jones-Irwin, 1985.

Zinsser, William. *On Writing Well.* Fifth Edition. New York: Harper Collins, 1994.

INDEX